CHEFS
OF THE PACIFIC NORTHWEST

Share

Because of seasonal or periodic changes in menus, the restaurants that you visit _may_ not be serving the recipes shared in this book. The recipes provided have each been proofed twice, but have not been kitchen tested by the author.

Bon Appétit !

Published and Distributed by

Graphic Arts
1006 Taft Street
Port Townsend, Washington 98368

Copyright © 1988 by Graphic Arts

International Standard Book Number: 0-969950-2-5

Published in the United States of America

Printed by Port Townsend Printing Company
Port Townsend, Washington 98368

Dedicated to
your gastronomic delight

While traveling and sketching, I met Serena Sinclair Lesley, a writer for many years covering the fashion field in both England and France, who now resides in Kalaloch, Washington. Serena impressed me with her knowledge of cooking also, and I feel fortunate that she had the time to write several of the introductions for the sections in my book.

Cover Restaurant: The Lido, Port Townsend, Washington
Cover art: Barbara Williams
Layout, type, art and production: Barbara Williams
Camera assistant: Toni Thomas
Proof reading: Serena Lesley
Shop assistant: Eva Riechel

Chefs sharing at....

Barbara Williams, graphic artist, teacher, caterer, comes to the Northwest from Monterey with a fresh eye and appreciative palate.

She felt, on moving to a Port Townsend hillside and converting a turn-of-the-century somewhat hippie house into an artist's handsome pad, a need here for a guide book that not only told you where to eat, but how it looked and what star recipes you could recreate in your own kitchen.

And so she's eaten her way around the Peninsula and beyond, both north and south of the Seattle area, sketching the while. Strictly in the interest of art and literature, she's put on thousands of miles and fifteen pounds in weight.

She is known in the California advertising world for her calligraphy, design work, and the process of turning faded old family photos into posterized serigraphs. This process was developed by Barbara during the years she was running a screen printing business. Already this newcomer to the region has been asked by restaurant owners to design menus, brochures and even decor.

Unlike some restaurant reviewers, this spunky, competent divorcee, mother of two, searches out the good in the restaurant world, and as she sketches, the restaurants become personal to her heart.

So she is hoping this book will steer you to new friends, spark you to revisit old favorites and spread general enjoyment for all.

Serena Lesley

About the book.....

I've fallen in love with Washington! Since moving here 1½ years ago, I have traveled around the western part of the state and marvel at the beauty that is around almost every turn of the road.

The idea for this book came partly from being treated so personally in several Port Townsend restaurants and partly because I love to sketch... so I put the two together (plus my love of eating out and also cooking) and this book just started "happening".

The first sketches were around Port Townsend, then a few in Sequim. How well I remember the night that I had a hard time going to sleep... I had laid out the beginning sketches and decided I just might have the makings for a book. I got so excited in thinking and planning, that it was after 4 a.m. before I finally got to sleep.

My work plan was to get up before the sun and start out...sketching and talking to restaurateurs. As I traveled further afield, it became necessary to stay overnight one night (occasionally two) and to be able to use the time more wisely, I could certainly have used more daylight for sketching in October and November.

By the end of October and into November the weather was occasionally not the best. I will never forget the extremely windy day that I passed a pickup truck just in time to see, from my rear view mirror, the camper top lifted by the wind and deposited about where my car would have been had I not passed when I did!

My travels took me first through the "banana belt" of Washington - Port Townsend and Sequim, then on to Port Angeles, the gateway to Victoria, B.C. via the Black Ball ferry. Highway west 101 from Port Angeles going south past Lake Crescent and Sol Duc. (As soon as this book has been completed, a trip to soak in the mineral pools at Sol Duc Resort will top my list of things to do.)
Now it's Forks and south... along the enchanting Rain Forest of the Olympic National Park.

I arrived at Kalaloch just before sunset and was treated to an incredible view of lines of evergreens silhouetted against a salmon-colored sky. The waves were rolling softly in, and the sinking sun was reflected on the crests of the waves. It was such a treat, that when I tried to explain the beauty to my mother and son, I gave up and decided that we would all spend a few days along the coast.

Late October and into November the news was all about the stock market problems, and I found it difficult to do much book business. I nearly lost hope. Then! New life! My daughter, Donna, gave birth to my second grandson, so the trip to California for this grand occasion occupied several weeks.

Along comes January and I'm back "on the road again"...down to Lake Quinault, Moclips and Ocean Shores... miles of flat beaches and windswept trees along the Pacific Ocean. A quick hop over to the south of Grays Harbor to visit Westport, then I headed east to Hoquiam that included a look at Hoquiam's Castle. Aberdeen nestles up to Hoquiam and is just over the river. A short distance east is the little town of Montesano with old buildings and a lot of history.

Several trips were necessary to Olympia where the city is abustle with Washington's business, and I found lots of charming places to dine. As I traveled back and forth, I was able to also stop off in Bremerton, Silverdale, Port Orchard, Allyn and Union.

By taking the ferry directly from Port Townsend, I visited Clinton, Langley, Oak Harbor and beyond to Anacortes. The ·Deception Pass Bridge and the surrounding area between Whidbey Island and the mainland beckoned... so a short stop to walk over the bridge and drink in all of the surrounding beauty was in order.

While in Anacortes the talk was all about the oil tanker that had just sunk, and I overheard snatches of the salvage crew's conversation at the table next to mine while I enjoyed a pleasant seafood lunch.

My son, Gene, who works at the Port Townsend Baking Company along with about a dozen other developmentally disabled adults*, by now is letting me know that he is ready for mom to be home every night. We have begun "countdown".· On the calendar Gene located the date for the book deadline and said, "Mom has only 5 weeks left"... then 4, 3 and so on. My plan for January and February was to be away overnight one night a week. This plan worked very well as I had many more

hours available this way.

A very special "Thank you" to my mother, Eva Riechel, for getting the breakfast for Gene and taking him to the bus stop for work on Thursdays; plus staying with him different evenings when I either had an extra night over-night or when I arrived home late occasionally.

Most Thursday nights I was fortun-ate in having Autumn Scott, Gene's boss at the bakery, sleep overnight in our guest room and be there to fix Gene's breakfast the next morning. Since she was attending a night class that ended too late for her to want to travel the extra hour back to her house, this arrangement worked to both of our ad-tages.

Because of the constraints of both time and space in the book, there were many towns and restaurants that had to be left "uncovered"...maybe I'll go again and do a second book! I <u>did</u> intentionally leave out the Seattle and surrounding areas, because there are already several books on this region.

What I have tried to do is include a few places in each area... some were historically interesting, some small and some informal, but the majority included are well recommended establishments that do an excellent job and have earned love and respect from their patrons.

Waiting for ferries becomes a common occurrence in summer and on weekends...but there can be pluses if you miss one ferry. My trip to Vashon Island was enjoyable, but when I arrived late one afternoon at the southernmost end of Vashon to catch the ferry to Tacoma, I had the misfortune to be the second car too many. I sat and fumed for about 5 minutes, then decided to get out and walk around a little.

Looking down at the beach from the parking area, I saw several clam diggers at work...with good results. I counted as many as 4 clams being taken from a single shovel of sand. There was also time to watch children playing on the shore...couples walking hand in hand...boats going by. So why was I in such a hurry? It was time to stop and "smell the roses".

A one day trip took me to LaConner just before the tulips bloomed, but there was a profusion of daffodils and crocus. The day I was in Everett began foggy, but soon cleared to reveal the sun-sparkled Port Susan.

Washington is a treat from the snow-covered mountains to the shores, the lakes and in the villages, towns and cities. There is something for everyone.

Great eating is a part of it all. I hope you find lots with the aid of my book.

Barbara Williams

* The Port Townsend Baking Company is a struggling non-profit business that enables many adults with developmental disabilities to earn a little and to put in many useful hours in constructive employment.
A visit shows the happiness and the enthusiasm that prevails here. If any of you should be looking for a top-notch place to make a charitable donation...this is it! Write to:

Bayshore Enterprises, Inc.
301 County Landfill Rd.
Port Townsend, WA 98368

Starting in the north, running along the Strait of Juan de Fuca, the zones in this book follow along the most traveled highways. In the cities the restaurants are listed alphabetically. You will find that it is worth seeking them out. Then when you are back home again, reading and cooking from the recipes in this book will bring back the joy of traveling throughout the beautiful Northwest portion of Washington state.

Note: If you are calling ahead for reservations, all of the restaurants in this book are in the 206 area. Hours shown could change.

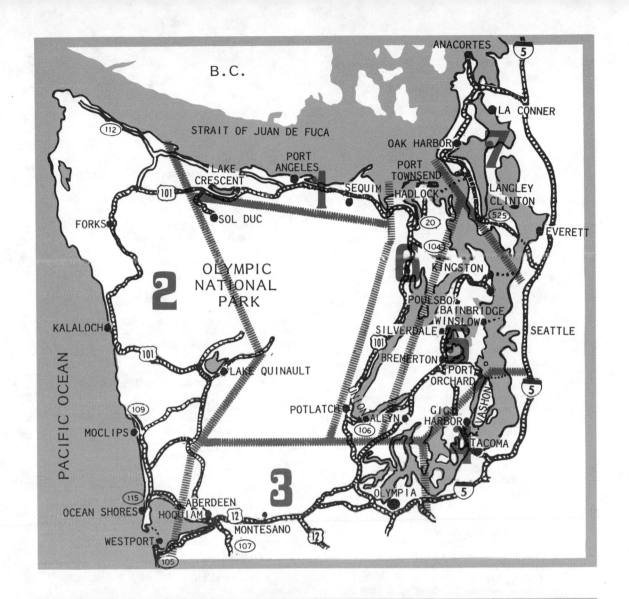

B.C.

STRAIT OF JUAN DE FUCA

OLYMPIC NATIONAL PARK

PACIFIC OCEAN

ANACORTES
LA CONNER
OAK HARBOR
PORT TOWNSEND
LANGLEY
CLINTON
LAKE CRESCENT
PORT ANGELES
SEQUIM
HADLOCK
EVERETT
FORKS
SOL DUC
KINGSTON
POULSBO
BAINBRIDGE
WINSLOW
SILVERDALE
SEATTLE
KALALOCH
BREMERTON
LAKE QUINAULT
PORT ORCHARD
POTLATCH
ALLYN
GIG HARBOR
VASHON
TACOMA
MOCLIPS
ABERDEEN
HOQUIAM
MONTESANO
OLYMPIA
OCEAN SHORES
WESTPORT

Page continuity in book: Section 1 is from east to west. Section 2 is north to south. Section 3 is west to east. Section 4, 5, and 6 are from south to north. Section 7 is from south Whidbey Island, north to Deception Pass, east to LaConner, then south on I-5 to Everett.

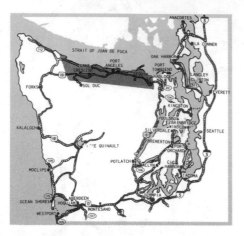

Like sisters, separated by only a few miles, Sequim and Port Angeles hug the coastline facing out to Canada. Sequim's the smiling, placid one, full of sunshine (it's rightly proud of its 17 inches of rain a year), while its brisker sister draws in people from all around to take courses at the good college, work in the mills and the helicopter company and the many attractive little shops.

They complement one another well. Sequim's one of the fast-growing retirement communities of the west, now choc-a-bloc with Californians who can't afford California and who have had their fill of freeways. The John Wayne marina's a beautiful lure for the sailing set and for those who love to simply sit and watch boat activity. Pottering around the Olympic Game Farm (where you may well see a Hollywood film crew at work) is another of Sequim's bucolic pleasures.

Hikers and skiers love Hurricane Ridge, and lazy sightseers too enjoy driving up its beautiful winding road behind the Park Service headquarters in Port Angeles to look out over the sea to Vancouver Island. Tempting? The ferry boat from Port Angeles to Victoria's an easy 90 minutes and some people go over for lunch and Shetlands. Charter fishing boats in Port Angeles virtually guarantee you a fine salmon haul from the Strait, the little community theatre has something on frequently, the college sponsors lunchtime readings (Peninsula writers are justly famous), and the high school auditorium hosts Port Angeles' excellent symphony several times a year. (Watch notices of what's on at the Coffee House or Port Angeles Music, both on First Street, or Thursday's issue of the Peninsula Daily News.)

You eat well in both communities, with emphasis, naturally, on locally caught seafood. Some of the most alluring meals are found on the easy 101 road that connects these two towns.... a drive calmed by many grazing cows and by the horses nibbling in their fields, the scent of sea on the one hand and the sight of snow-capped mountains on the other.

SL

SECTION 1

SEQUIM: Casoni's, The Oak Table, The Old Sequim Depot
PORT ANGELES: The Bushwhacker, C'est Si Bon, The Coffee
    House, The Greenery, Granny's, Hickory Dock, The
    Landing, The Log Cabin

Cooking any type of fresh pasta is quicker than dry pasta, and there is a definite improvement in taste and texture.

COOKING PASTA

1. To boiling, unsalted water add 1 lb. of fresh pasta.
2. Separate with pasta fork to promote even cooking.
3. Just bring back to a boil and then drain and put in skillet with 4 oz. olive oil and toss with garlic, a little basil, pepper and salt to taste.
4. Serve immediately topped with favorite cheese, or re-heat in skillet just before serving, adding a little chicken or clam stock to keep moist.

Seafood is great with pasta or <u>in</u> pasta, try the following:

GAMBERETTI PATRICIA

3 tablespoons olive oil
1 pound small bay shrimp
1 cup dry Chablis
1 cup half and half
1 teaspoon chopped garlic
2 tablespoons chopped parsley
½ teaspoon marjoram
½ cup diced fresh tomatoes
1 pound cooked fresh linguine or fettucine pasta,
    prepared as described above.

Procedure

In a non-stick sauté pan or cast iron skillet, heat oil and add garlic, shrimp and marjoram. Toss lightly to heat and add wine.

Allow wine to reduce slightly, then add half and half and parsley.

Bring to a light boil, then add cooked pasta and tomatoes. Toss lightly.

Put into serving platter and top with cheese.   Serves 4.

Casoni's Restaurant was established
on the 4ᵗʰ of July, 1984 in a former
Seafirst Bank building at the intersection of Carlsborg & Highway
101 just 3 miles west of downtown Sequim.
They specialize in progressive Italian cuisine utilizing home-made
fresh pasta for the day's customers.

From Memorial Day thru Labor Day: Open every day from 4 p.m.
Rest of the year: Open Wednesday thru Sunday.

KORYUFFINS

8 fresh mushrooms
4 strips thickly sliced bacon
　　or 8 strips thinly sliced bacon
16 large fresh spinach leaves

2 English muffins
4 eggs
4 ounces shredded Swiss cheese
3 tablespoons clarified butter or
　　peanut oil

To start, poach eggs and toast muffins.
Meanwhile, start bacon cooking and slice mushrooms. When bacon is medium-rare, remove from heat and cut into 1" square pieces.

Sauté mushrooms in 3 tablespoons clarified butter (peanut oil is optional). When mushrooms are soft, drain oil and add bacon. Stir and cook 15 seconds and avoid browning very much. Set aside.

Julienne spinach and blanch lightly.

Lay toasted muffins open-faced on 2 plates and sprinkle 1½ ounces of cheese on each, followed by blanched mushrooms and bacon, followed by blanched spinach.

Top with poached eggs. Sprinkle lightly with remaining cheese.

(Hollandaise sauce topping and hashbrowns on the side are suggested.)

EGGS NICOLE

2 croissants
8 fresh mushrooms, sliced
¼ medium onion, diced
16 large fresh spinach leaves,
　　chopped

6 large eggs
½ teaspoon all purpose seasoned salt
6 ounces shredded Swiss cheese
1 tablespoon dry Florio Marsala wine
　　(or cooking sherry)

Toast croissants and center on two plates in a circular fashion.
Scramble eggs in a bowl and set aside.

Using 3 tablespoons of clarified butter (or peanut oil), sauté mushrooms and onions until soft. Drain oil and add seasoned salt, spinach and wine. Mix well.

Add eggs and scramble together until well blended. Add cheese and scramble until desired consistency is reached.

Place scramble mixture on top of croissant.

Hollandaise sauce topping and hash browns on the side are suggested.

Nestled in the Dungeness valley
is Sequim's best kept secret... the Oak Table Cafe.
Opened 7 years ago by Mary and Billy Nagler, the Oak Table offers a wide
selection of hand crafted breakfasts and lunches. Fresh squeezed orange
and grapefruit juices are served - fresh cream and butter are used.

From the second you step in the door, you'll see the care that's gone
into preparing a unique dining experience.

The friendly service and quaint cottage atmosphere add to the irresistible
food that keeps the locals and tourists flocking back.

Open: Mon. - Sat. 7 a.m. till 3 p.m.   Lunch only Mon.- Fri. 11 till 3 p.m.
        Sunday 8 a.m. till 3 p.m.

MOCHA PECAN PIE

pastry for 8" or 9" pie
¼ cup butter
¾ cup sugar
1 teaspoon vanilla
2 tablespoons flour
4 eggs

¼ cup melted chocolate
¼ cup coffee liqueur
½ cup dark corn syrup
¾ cup evaporated milk
1 cup pecans (chopped or whole)

Line pie plate with pastry. Chill. Set oven at 400°. Cream together butter, sugar, vanilla and flour. Mix well. Beat in eggs, one at a time. Stir in chocolate, coffee liqueur, corn syrup, evaporated milk and pecans. Mix well, and pour into pie pan. Bake for 10 minutes. Reduce heat to 325° and bake until firm (approximately 40 minutes). Garnish with whipped cream and pecans if you wish.

GLAZED CARROTS AND PINEAPPLE

4 large sliced carrots (2½ cups)
¾ teaspoon salt
½ cup water
½ cup pineapple tidbits with
    syrup drained from can

1 tablespoon cornstarch
½ cup light corn syrup
2 tablespoons butter

Cook carrots with salt and water, covered until barely tender. Drain any remaining liquid into a measuring cup, then add pineapple syrup to measure 1 cup in all; mix with cornstarch in saucepan. Cook stirring constantly until thickened and clear. Stir in corn syrup and butter. Add carrots and pineapple bits. Heat.

The Old Depot Restaurant, located in the Sequim Railroad Depot, was originally built in 1916 when the trains were shipping lumber from Port Townsend to Port Angeles. From 1960 the trains carried only freight, till 1984 when all services stopped and the building sat empty. Recently Roy and Marilyn Baker purchased the rundown depot and restored the building, adding a large dining area, a deck and a theatre. Dinner shows are frequently held.

The menu offers a wide selection of seafoods, chicken, beef and pastas.

Open: Wed.- Sat. 11:30 a.m. till 10:00 p.m.
Sun. noon till 5:00 p.m.

BUSHWHACKER OYSTERS ROCKEFELLER

5 to 6 ounces chopped bacon
½ lb. chopped spinach
2 tablespoons chopped parsley
¼ cube butter
½ tablespoon chopped garlic
salt to taste

dash of Tabasco
cayenne pepper to taste
¼ cup ground Ritz cracker crumbs
2 dozen extra small oysters
3 lemons
2 pounds rock salt

On low heat, melt butter, garlic. Then add spinach, parsley, Tabasco, cayenne, salt. Cook on low heat for about 8 - 10 minutes. Set aside, fold in cracker crumbs, let cool.

Shuck half of oyster shell, put ¼ of an inch of rock salt in baking dish. (It's best to cook and serve on same dish, because it's hard to handle when hot.)

Lay oysters in halfshell on your baking dish on bed of salt. Put a nice covering of stuffing over each one. Then cover with cheese and top with bacon.

Bake 400° until bacon is browned. Garnish with lemon wedges and parsley.

BUSHWHACKER CAJUN SHRIMP

Seasoning mixture

¼ cup seasoning salt
5 tablespoons paprika
2 tablespoons cayenne pepper
1½ tablespoons dried onion
   (or onion powder)

½ tablespoon ground cumin
½ tablespoon ground coriander
½ tablespoon marjoram leaf
½ tablespoon fennel seed
1½ tablespoons dried garlic
   (or garlic powder)

Combine the above ingredients in a blender, blend until powder. Keep this in a salt shaker for easy use.

Ingredients

shrimp for 6 to 8 people: 4 pounds shelled 41/50 shrimp
¼ cup white wine
2 tablespoons garlic
¼ cube butter

Simmer butter, wine and garlic in a large skillet till done. Drain all liquid except approximately 4 tablespoons. Sprinkle heavy coat of seasoning mixture and stir shrimp over medium heat for about two minutes.

Note: Salt and cayenne might be cut back according to taste.

The Bushwhacker Restaurant migrated from the wilds of Montana in the spring of 1976. Since arriving on the Strait of Juan de Fuca shores, they've developed a menu centered on the fresh seafood of local waters. In Montana they were well-known for corn-fed prime rib and charbroiled steaks.

Their chef, Mike Wiley, has done wonders with Washington seafood, and the owners, Julie and Robert Grattan, hope you'll find this out for yourself.

TOURNEDOS ROYAL   For 4 persons

clarified butter
4 tournedos of beef *
8 ounces of crab meat
4 ounces heavy cream

2 ounces dry vermouth
salt and pepper
2 ounces cognac
strong beef stock

* Tournedos are cut from the heart of the
  filet of beef.

Dry tournedos on paper towels. Place 3 tablespoons of clarified butter in the skillet and set over moderately high heat. When butter is hot enough, sear tournedos for 2 or 3 minutes all around.

Meanwhile, in another skillet, reduce $\frac{1}{3}$ its volume, 4 ounces heavy cream, 2 ounces dry vermouth, salt, pepper to taste.

Add crab and turn off the heat, so it just stays warm.

Sear tournedos, set each on a hot plate. Arrange crab on top. Pour 2 ounces strong beef stock in skillet in which tournedos were cooked, reduce it at high heat. Add 2 ounces cognac, reduce 1 more minute, pour over crab.

ALMOND TARTE

Paté Brisée Sucré

2 cups flour
5 ounces butter

2 tablespoons sugar
2 to 3 tablespoons ice water

Cut butter into small pieces in the flour. Add sugar and mix till flaky. Add water and mix again and form into ball. Set aside.

Filling

2 cups heavy cream
2 cups sliced almonds
1 cup ground walnuts
2 cups sugar

2 tablespoons vanilla
1 teaspoon almond extract

Mix all filling ingredients and let rest for 2 hours.

After forming your shell over a removable tart form, pre-bake the shell in 350° oven. When shell is cool, add filling and bake in 375° oven for about 1 hour.   Serve cold.

Ceiling to floor windows serve as a frame to C'est Si Bon's view of their rose gardens and the Olympic mountains in the distance. In season, the roses bloom profusely in a myriad of colors.

The main dining room is pleasing—light walls set off a good collection of paintings.

Norbert and Michele Jukasz (from Lyons via Malibu) feature many French recipes as well as seafood, beef and lamb specialties...escargot and oyster appetizers, etc.

But try to save room for one of their outstanding desserts.

ORIENTAL SALAD

Slice thinly and on the diagonal:
white cabbage, celery, green pepper, green onion, chopped parsley.
Toss together gently.

<u>Sesame ginger dressing</u>

Blend together:
2 tablespoons grated fresh ginger   dash of each of the following:
2 cups safflower oil   sugar, garlic powder, onion powder,
½ cup vinegar   salt and ginger powder.
2 tablespoons sesame oil   apple juice or crushed pineapple to taste.

COFFEE CAKE

<u>Mix together</u>   1 cup raisins
3 cups flour   2 teaspoons baking soda
1 cup brown sugar   ½ teaspoon each of ginger,
½ cup white sugar   cinnamon and salt
1 cup chopped walnuts   ¼ teaspoon cloves

<u>Add</u>   1 cup oil
2 large apples (grated)   3 beaten eggs
1 cup apple sauce   2 tablespoons vinegar

Put into greased and floured 9 x 13" pan. Bake at 350° for approximately 1½ hours.

The Coffee House Restaurant and Gallery offers a unique atmosphere which surrounds you with magical sculptures and art.

The foods are freshly prepared with quality ingredients ranging from the most wholesome to the utmost decadent!

It's a small cozy place, and they bring in local musicians to entertain on Friday evenings.

BRAISED RED CABBAGE

3 tablespoons olive oil
2 lbs red cabbage (sliced)

1 med. onion
   (Julienne style)

Clean cabbage of tough leaves, cut cabbage in half (through core). Remove core, cut cabbage halves into quarters, then to $\frac{1}{4}$ inch thick pieces.

Heat olive oil in lg. heavy bottom pot at med. high temp. Sauté onion until transparent. Add cabbage. cook until wilted.

Add next 4 ingred., cook 15-20 min., stir often. Salt, pepper to taste.

4 ingredient list

2 whole cloves (crushed)
3 tablespoons red wine vinegar

3 tablespoons sugar
$\frac{1}{2}$ cup applesauce (unsweetened)

Salt and fresh ground pepper to taste. Serves approx. six.

FETTUCCINE SALSICCIA

1 lb. fresh fettuccine
8 ounces butter

eight ingredient list

1 tablespoon fresh chopped garlic
12 - 15 mushroom caps
$\frac{1}{2}$ medium onion(Julienne style)
1 bunch green onions sliced
   (use first 4 " only)
$\frac{1}{2}$ med. green pepper (Julienne style)

2 cooked Italian sausage links
   (2 to 3 ounces each)
   sliced $\frac{1}{4}$ inch thick
1 teaspoon sweet basil
1 teaspoon oregano

for sauce reduction

4 ounces white wine
12 ounces heavy cream
4 ounces butter

6 ounces parmesan cheese
   (grated)
salt and white pepper to taste

Bring 1 gallon water to full boil in large pot, add fettuccine, stir. Then reduce to low boil and cook 12 minutes, till done. Noodles should be limp, but firm. Drain and rinse in cold water.

In 12" sauté pan, melt 4 ounces butter on med. high heat. Next add the 10 ingredients, sauté lightly approx. 3-5 minutes. Add white wine, sauté until wine reduces to a third of its volume.

Add cream and 4 oz. butter, bring back to boil till cream reduces to sauce thickness. Salt, pepper to taste. While cream is reducing, reheat pasta in hot water bath, drain.When cream is reduced to sauce thickness, add 6 oz. parmesan cheese and pasta, toss thoroughly.
Serve on four heated plates, top with grated parmesan cheese.

The Greenery Restaurant is quaintly located off the street in downtown Port Angeles, with the entrance near the alley.

A large selection of traditional and specialty items is offered for breakfast.
For lunch - salads galore, sandwiches, homemade pastas and sautéed dishes.
A sophisticated dinner menu offers a variety of homemade pastas, beef, veal and poultry dishes.... with a Northern Italian flair. Their selection of seafood is one of the largest in the area.

Dave and Marsha Reynolds stated that they are intent on pleasing you with the best service possible.

VERA CRUZ STYLE RED SNAPPER

Sauté chopped onion, minced garlic, chopped canned tomatoes, bell peppers in oil until soft. Add small amount chili powder, black pepper to taste, salt, cumin and thyme.

Dredge white fish in flour, then in milk-egg mixture, then again in flour. Deep fry till golden brown.

Arrange on platter, pour sauce over, sprinkle with shredded cheese and then melt cheese under oven broiler. Garnish with chopped cilantro.

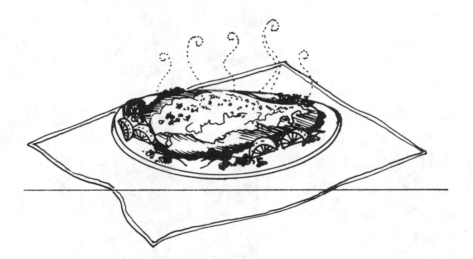

NACHOS

Mince and sauté one diced onion and tomato. Sauté until soft. When soft, add shredded cheese and stir until melted.

Pour mixture over corn chips that you have kept warm. Garnish with peppers, guacomole and salsa.

Hickory Dock is just completing....not a face-lift... but a totally rebuilt restaurant. The decor is Northwest sea coast with old pioneer pictures decorating the walls.

John said his is the "farthest west pit bar-b-que on the mainland USA!"

As you enter the restaurant, you'll enter the new gift shop first.... featuring Northwest Arts and Crafts.

The house specialty is the real pit bar-b-que, and there's seafood and sandwiches.... also daily specials.

The restaurant is located across the street and down a few doors from the ferries going to Victoria, B.C.

PICKLED SHRIMP IN BEER

2 to 3 pounds (16 to 20) shrimp in shell
¼ cup pickling spice
2 quarts beer (1 six-pack, or use
      stale draft beer)
2 to 3 drops Tabasco (optional)

Bring beer, pickling spice and Tabasco to a boil. Drop in shrimp and
return to a boil. Drain shrimp in a colander. Cool to refrigerator temperature. Either serve as individual servings on lettuce-lined salad plate
or bowl, at least 6 to 8 per person, or put in a large bowl and everyone shares. Garnish with lettuce and lemon.

(You may wish to serve with hot clarified butter or a tangy cocktail
sauce, but it's not really necessary.)

A great white wine and the shared activity of each guest shelling their
shrimp to eat makes for a great party.....expensive, but memorable!

SALMON BISQUE

4 tablespoons butter
1 small onion, finely minced
4 tablespoons flour (or
    1 tablespoon arrowroot)
2 teaspoons salt (omit 1 teaspoon if
    using part smoked salmon)
¼ teaspoon pepper (or 1 or 2 drops
    of Tabasco)
2 cups whole milk ⎫
2 cups half and half ⎭ scalded

1 cup canned salmon (or left-over
    baked or poached)
          or
¼ cup cooked salmon & ¼ cup
    finely flaked smoked salmon
1 pkg frozen green peas in butter
    sauce
whipped cream

Melt butter, add onion and simmer 5 minutes...do not brown! Blend in
flour (or arrowroot), salt and pepper (or Tabasco). Add hot scalded milk
gradually, stirring constantly. Heat to boiling and cook 3 to 5 minutes.

Add finely flaked warm salmon and peas to milk mixture and serve at
once. Garnish with dollop of whipped cream accented with fresh parsley
sprig and lightly dusted with paprika.   Serves 6 to 8.

The Landing's Fish and Burger Bar is located just behind the Chamber of Commerce building in the Lincoln Landing waterfront shopping mall. This popular restaurant is an attractive and informal place, where you may order freshly-caught seafood or char-broiled hamburgers. Other entrées include broiled NW salmon, crab, shrimp Louies, great fish and chips, Juan de Fuca clam chowder, steamed clams and Hood Canal oysters.... and the prices are moderate. The service is fast, in case you're waiting for the ferry to Victoria, B.C. (The ferry docks just next door.)

Open every day from 7 a.m. till 8 p.m. Summer and winter hours may vary.

phone 452-2016

CHILI BEANS

4 cups small red beans
4 large tablespoons chili powder
1 teaspoon oregano
½ teaspoon garlic powder
½ teaspoon onion powder
1 teaspoon M.S.G.
½ tablespoon salt

½ tablespoon pepper
1 teaspoon cumin
1 medium onion, chopped
1 heaping tablespoon prepared mustard
1 pound hamburger
1 large can tomato sauce

Soak beans in water overnight. Drain water off next day.
Fry onion and hamburger together, stirring.
Add all ingredients together and cook on low heat for 1 to 2 hours.
Stir occasionally.
Good with shredded **cheddar cheese** sprinkled on top of chili.

ARTICHOKE CHICKEN

2 whole chicken breasts
seasoned salt
1 jar 6 oz. marinated artichoke hearts
1 teaspoon flour
½ cup water

¼ cup dry white wine
1 chicken bouillon cube (crumbled)
12 fresh mushrooms, cut in half
1 tablespoon chopped parsley

Bone chicken breasts, discard skin. Sprinkle with seasoned salt. Heat 3 teaspoons of artichoke marinade in skillet and brown chicken slowly on all sides. Drain off all but 1 teaspoon of marinade. Push chicken to one side and stir in flour. Add water and bouillon, stir until mixture boils and thickens.

Add mushrooms and artichoke hearts. Slop sauce over chicken. Cover and simmer over low heat about 50 minutes or until chicken is tender. Sprinkle with chopped parsley.

Shown here is the outdoor covered patio at Granny's.... a great spot in the summer months. There are 2 aviaries of doves to entertain you while you eat. You're likely to find one or more trucks parked in front, as well as a large number of "regulars" plus those passing through.
Granny is often there to greet you; or her brother, Richard, is there.
The place is very informal. (Try the "Granny Breakfast" or "Granny Burger".)

Open seven days a week for breakfast, lunch and dinner.

MUD PIE Serves 8

3 boxes Nabisco chocolate cookie wafers
1½ cubes butter
3 gallons ice cream

Hershey chocolate syrup
whipping cream
maraschino cherries

Crust: Roll out chocolate cookies to fine crumbs. Melt butter and mix together. Mixture should hold firm when pressed in hand. Spray spring pan 9" x 3" high with Pam or other vegetable food spray. Press crumb mixture on sides and bottom. Freeze for 1 hour.

Pie: Soften ice cream (suggested Mocha Almond Fudge or Mint Chocolate Chip) or flavor of your choice. Pack ice cream into spring pan and mound high in the center. Freeze for 24 hours (or longer) before serving.

> Note: When proofing this recipe, the staff couldn't believe that a pie with 3 gallons of ice cream and 3 boxes of cookies could be eaten by only 8 people, so a phone call was made to Bette Linenkugel at the Log Cabin Resort Restaurant. Bette laughed and said that often customers share one piece.

GEODUC A King clam, native of Puget Sound

geoduc (tenderized and pounded)
eggs
flour
sliced almonds
butter

lemon wedges
tartar sauce

Allow 6 to 8 ounces of geoduc per person.

Dip each piece of geoduc in beaten eggs, then lightly flour. Sauté geoduc in butter for approximately 2½ minutes, medium heat on each side.

Sprinkle almonds on top and serve with lemon wedges and tartar sauce.

Note: Geoduc is pronounced "Gooey Duck".

The original Log Cabin Resort, built in 1895 by a Mr. Saunders, was a handsome two-story building of peeled cedar logs. It fell victim to fire in 1932, and the present lodge was built by Carl Hansen.

It has expanded over the years and presently includes cabins, motel rooms, A-frame chalets, R.V. and camping sites, store, gift shop, marina and boat rentals, restaurant and bar.

In 1938, under the Roosevelt administration, Congress set aside this area (which now covers just over 1,000,000 acres) as a National Park. In 1982 the Olympic National Park was added to the list of World Heritage Sites.

The Log Cabin Resort occupies 17 acres in the park and is located on the sunny side of Lake Crescent.

The restaurant overlooks Lake Crescent and the mountains beyond.

The restaurant is open seasonally.

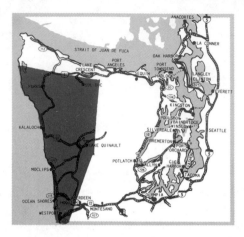

You could almost, looking at the map of 101 as it scissors along the Pacific coastline, think of taking survival rations, or at the very least, a picnic.

But don't. There are agreeable places to eat along this glorious route: you just have to grab one while you're there....otherwise, it's a long hungry 35 mile haul to the next one.

Get relaxed and soothed for your drive by soaking in the hot spring outdoor pools at Sol Duc Resort...you can take a meal there, too. Then it's on to Forks, a tough little town with a spunky spirit all its own, proudly proclaiming itself "logging capitol of the world" by a spliced-off cedar on display on the main street, and a great totem pole nearby opposite Tillicum Park. Stop here for your rugged fishing and hiking gear... it's the real thing... and perhaps a clam license as well, then eat a sturdy filling meal.

Drive past the entrance road to Hoh Rain Forest, a magic storylike place with informative well-marked nature trails of varying lengths, past the entry to the Cottonwood camping area.

Reach the sea at Ruby Beach, then Kalaloch, unwind on a beach walk, explore wondrous tidepools teeming with starfish, and take a meal in Kalaloch's coffee shop or restaurant. Then it's on through the village of Queets, home of many Quinault tribal members, and the road slopes inland past logging mills and wild country to Amanda Park.

This little settlement's turn-off point to idyllic Lake Quinault with its boating, fishing, swimming and pleasant eating. Then it's on through the cozy, solid little village of Neilton, then Humptulips. Here's where you part from 101, but in a good cause: the sea.

It's a glorious bit of cross-country, rolling past villages like Copalis Crossing with its surprisingly huge supermarket and off-beat gift shop in an old jail. Turn right for handsome Ocean Crest Resort with its health spa, turn left for blowy Ocean Shores, its miles of flat beaches sturdy enough for the dune buggies you rent there, its interlaced canals tranquil for bird-watchers and canoers.

Charter boats, for fishing or just leisurely whale-spotting, wait for you at Westport (in summertime via a foot ferry from Ocean Shores, otherwise a winding drive to Aberdeen and on).

SL

SECTION 2

SOL DUC: Sol Duc Hot Springs Resort
FORKS: Clark's Vagagond
KALALOCH: Kalaloch Lodge
QUINAULT: Lake Quinault Lodge,   Rainforest Restaurant
MOCLIPS: Ocean Crest Lodge
OCEAN SHORES: Homeport, Polynesian
WESTPORT: Arthur's

BAKED RED SNAPPER FLORENTINE

4 8-ounce red snapper filets	1 tablespoon capers
2 tablespoons olive oil	2 tablespoons butter
¼ teaspoon coarse black pepper	1 teaspoon dijon mustard
½ cup fresh lemon juice	1 bunch fresh spinach

1. Place snapper filets in baking pan.
2. In a small bowl mix together olive oil, dijon mustard, pepper and ½ of the lemon juice. Drizzle mixture over the fish evenly covering each filet.
3. Wash spinach thoroughly, removing the stems. Drain well. Place spinach on cutting board and cut fine (shred like coleslaw).
4. Bake fish in 400° oven for 10 - 12 minutes. (Do not overcook).
5. Cover half of each plate with bed of shredded spinach.
6. Remove cooked fish from oven, placing one filet on each bed of spinach, careful to save juices in pan.
7. Add butter, capers and the rest of lemon juice to pan fish was cooked in. Stir all juices together and spoon over fish. Serve at once.

Serve with sliced fresh fruit or steamed vegetables.
Fresh shredded spinach eliminates the need for rice or potato.

Serves 4.

CRAB STILTON

12 ounces Dungeness crab (legs and body meat)
20 to 24 mushroom caps (blanched in boiling water with ½ of lemon)
4 tablespoons chopped green onions
4 ounces Stilton cheese, crumbled
24 grapes (green seedless) halved
4 tablespoons herb butter (recipe below)

Herb butter

4 tablespoons butter	¼ teaspoon fresh grated nutmeg
juice from half lemon	1 tablespoon fresh parsley, chopped fine
2 teaspoons fresh tarragon (or ½ teaspoon dried)	¼ teaspoon fresh ground black pepper

1. In an individual ramekin or scallop shell place 5 or 6 mushroom caps (bottom side up). Sprinkle 3 ounces of crab over mushrooms. Add onions, grapes, crumbled cheese and herb butter.
2. Place ramekins on a cookie sheet. Bake in 375° oven for 10 to 12 minutes.

Variation: Oysters may be substituted for crab meat.

Sol Duc is located in the Olympic National Park 42 miles west of Port Angeles....the drive in from Highway 101 is beautiful.... moss covered trees, a river running along side the road, and a good chance you'll see elk. The Sol Duc Hot Springs offer fine dining, overnight lodging, swimming, hiking, camping and the legendary hot mineral waters for your relaxing pleasure.

Legend has it that the waters have healing qualities, so go see for yourself!

Open seasonally.

CLARK'S GLAZED CHICKEN

8 skinless chicken breasts
1 cup orange marmalade
¾ cup Madeira wine

1 tablespoon tarragon leaves
melted butter

Place chicken in shallow pan, lightly brush with butter, put in oven at 325° for about 1 hour. Baste very often with mixture of marmalade, wine and tarragon until chicken is well glazed and lightly browned and done. Serves 8.

TASTY SAUTÉ OF SOLE

2 to 3 pounds sole filets
salt
fresh grated nutmeg
flour
½ cup butter
1 cup heavy cream

Sprinkle fish with salt and nutmeg, dust with flour.

Sauté in wide frying pan in butter over medium heat until lightly browned.

Transfer fish to serving dish and keep warm.

Stir cream into pan and boil over high heat stirring until light golden brown in color, and thickened. Drizzle over fish and serve immediately.

Any other white fish may also be used in place of the sole.

Serves 8.

Clark's Vagabond Restaurant is a casual place where Forks folk like to meet and eat. Claude Clark said he's been in business for over 30 years ! He said it's a family run endeavor and he's proud of the fact that so much is made right on the premises.... pies, soups, salads, many entrees, and specials.

Open: 7 days a week. Mon.-Thurs. 5 a.m. till 10 p.m.
Fri. & Sat. open 24 hours. Sunday till 9 p.m.

SALMON BISQUE

Seasoning ingredients

3 tablespoons butter
2 tablespoons chopped celery
¼ cup chopped mushrooms
2 chopped carrots
1 chopped medium onion

2 small bay leaves
1 sprig marjoram
few grains of nutmeg
½ teaspoon ground peppercorn
½ teaspoon salt

Place ingredients above in deep pan. Cook slowly for 5 minutes.

Ingredients

1 cup flaked, cooked salmon
1 teaspoon lemon juice
2 cups chicken stock

1 cup heavy cream or milk
   (not ice cold)
dash sherry or white wine

Add to seasoning mixture, lemon juice and chicken stock. Simmer for 15 minutes. Then add salmon and cook for 5 minutes.

Just before serving, add 1 cup heavy cream or milk. Add a dash of dry sherry or white wine if desired.

LEMON MOUSSE

1 envelope unflavored gelatin
½ cup fresh lemon juice
4 eggs, separated
1½ cups granulated sugar
⅛ teaspoon of salt

3 tablespoons butter
rind of one lemon grated
1 teaspoon vanilla extract
1 cup of heavy cream

Soften gelatin in lemon juice and set aside. In top of double boiler beat the egg yolks, adding 1 cup of sugar, a small amount at a time until thick. Add the gelatin lemon mixture, salt and butter.

Cook stirring constantly over hot, NOT boiling, water until thick (takes about 8-10 minutes). Remove from heat, stir in lemon rind and vanilla. Cook until mixture begins to stiffen.

In separate bowl, beat egg whites until very soft peaks form, add the remaining ½ cup of sugar a small amount at a time, beat to stiff peaks.

In a separate bowl, beat the cream stiff, fold the egg whites and whipped cream into the lemon mixture.

Put into individual serving dishes, refrigerate at least 4 hours and garnish with whipped cream.

Serves 8.

You could be distracted from your fine meal by one of 3 things: a passing whale, a wandering Soviet trawler, Pacific waves flinging giant logs like matchsticks up the ever-changing Kalaloch Creek below your eyes.

But the view — one of the Peninsula's most magical — from those bay windows is nicely complemented by seafood dinners the guests insist upon. Kalaloch was first on the Peninsula with cajun-spiced blackened salmon, and it's still a favorite.

Chef Howard Kelley does a great salmon bisque as well. The usual standards are available: steaks, sole, shrimp Louie salad, home-baked pies.... but no pastas, no "slimmer" dishes. New... daily vegetarian dish. Good list of Washington wines.

Open year around. 7:30 a.m. till 9 p.m.

SAUTÉED BARBECUED PRAWNS

2 tablespoons butter
pinch of oregano
pinch of basil
6 prawns 16/20 size

Sauté prawns and flip over.
Add:
¼ cup chopped onions
¼ cup mushrooms
1 teaspoon fresh garlic chopped

Sauté till mushrooms are cooked (two to three minutes).
Add 2 ounces of Nalley's barbecue sauce and sauté till sauce is hot.

BAKED SALMON

¼ cup white wine
¼ fresh lemon (squeezed)
2 tablespoons butter reduced (melted)

2 tablespoons capers
salmon

Put the salmon meat side down, poach in wine and butter and lemon juice and flip. (One half minute for each side.)
Sprinkle 2 tablespoons capers on top.

Using same pan, bake in oven 450° about ten minutes. (This depends on the thickness of the cut.) Cook till done.

From the moment you step into the immense lobby, dominated by the massive fireplace, you sense the quiet elegance, leisured atmosphere of yesteryears.

You will dine on superb food as you gaze out over Lake Quinault..... amid the spectacular scenery of the Olympic Rain Forest, with the mountains soaring upward on every side.

Enjoy the peaceful charm and 62-year-old Main Lodge, indoor swimming, jacuzzi and sauna.

Nearby - for active outdoor pleasure, there is hiking, boating and fishing.

Open year around.

CHINESE BARBECUED PORK

2 pork tenderloins
¼ cup honey
½ cup burgundy
⅓ cup soy sauce
½ teaspoon cinnamon

¼ teaspoon celery seed
2 cloves garlic, crushed
¼ cup onion, sliced
¼ cup brown sugar
1 teaspoon red food coloring

Cut fat from tenderloins and set aside. Mix remaining ingredients together in a large bowl. Coat tenderloins with sauce and leave them in the sauce overnight in refrigerator.

When ready to cook, preheat oven to 350°. Put tenderloins on a baking rack, making sure each piece doesn't touch the other. Bake for 45 minutes. Check for doneness by cutting a small slit in the middle of the tenderloin and look for redness. When done, let cool and cut into thin pieces. Serve with sesame seed, catsup and hot mustard.

STEAK KIEV

2 pounds top sirloin
½ cup butter
2 tablespoons garlic, crushed
½ cup onion, finely chopped

1 tablespoon parsley, chopped
½ teaspoon white pepper
½ teaspoon salt

Slice steak thinly across the grain. Mix butter, garlic, onion, parsley, white pepper and salt. Heat sauté pan over medium high heat. When pan is hot, add steak pieces to pan in one layer. Then add butter mixture, cook until meat is seared (approximately 2 minutes) and flip meat. Cook until desired doneness (approximately 2 minutes) and remove from pan. Make sure to cover the meat with butter mixture in pan.

Serves 4.

The Rain Forest Restaurant is part of the Rain Forest Resort Village located on the south shore of Lake Quinault. What makes this nice is that they offer so much: fireplace cabins, a village inn, RV campground, lounge, general store and boating. While there, go take a look at the "world's largest" Sitka Spruce tree.... located on the resort grounds.

The view of the lake is outstanding and the sunsets are breathtaking! So bring the whole family — there's a wide variety of dinners... from spaghetti to steak and lobster... all prepared to order.

Open year - round.

FLORENTINE SALMON

2 tablespoons butter
1 cup sliced fresh mushrooms
½ cup chopped green onions
½ bunch fresh spinach
1 ounce brandy
4 salmon filets (8 ounces each)
½ cup white wine

Quickly sauté mushrooms, green onions and spinach in butter, then add brandy, flame and remove from heat.

Cut pocket in salmon filets and stuff with the sauté mixture above.

Place salmon in pan and season to taste with salt and pepper.

Add ½ cup of white wine.

Bake in 450° oven for 10 to 12 minutes, depending on the thickness of the salmon filets.

Serves 4.

The Ocean Crest Resort has it all! Exceptional dining with spectacular panoramas of the Pacific Ocean in a natural forest setting ...... from the cliff-top vantage whirlpool, comfortable rooms and apartments with cozy fireplaces, large indoor heated pool, hair salon, sauna, exercise room, sun decks, meeting facilities and lounge.

SEAFOOD SAUTÉ

6 or 7 pieces of cubed firm white fish
    (such as cod or halibut)
2 prawns
2 oysters (extra small)
2 or 3 scallops (depends on size)
½ teaspoon seasoning salt
½ cup sliced mushrooms

2 tablespoons diced green pepper
2 tablespoons diced red pepper
2 tablespoons green onions
sherry wine
clarified butter

Place 2 tablespoons of clarified butter in sauté pan. Add the diced green and red pepper, green onions and mushrooms. (Be sure to put your onion and pepper mix in butter first, so that the flavor marries with the sauté.)

Cook until prawns and fish are white and firm. When sauté is almost done, add approximately 3 teaspoons sherry and flame. Cook about 1 minute after adding wine to reduce sauce. Transfer to serving dish.

Makes 1 serving.

CHILLED HALIBUT STEAK with baby bay shrimp, lemon cheese sauce

2 pounds halibut steaks or fresh
   halibut cut into 8 oz. pieces
¼ pound shrimp
3 egg yolks
⅔ cup milk

8 oz. shredded cheddar cheese
2 tablespoons lemon pepper
2 tablespoons lemon juice
1 teaspoon chicken base

In top of double boiler, beat egg yolks and milk until blended. Cook, stirring constantly until thickened. Add cheese, lemon pepper, lemon juice and chicken base.

Heat until cheese is melted, then cover and set aside.

Dredge halibut in flour. Grill in 2 tablespoons of oil until firm and white. Heat shrimp by dipping in boiling water for a few seconds until hot. Reheat sauce if necessary.

Place shrimp on top of halibut and spoon sauce over the top of both. Makes 4 servings.

Consistency is the word that best describes the Home Port. This attractive restaurant, located on Pt. Brown Avenue just inside the entrance to Ocean Shores, is known for great food, reasonable prices and pleasant decor. Fresh seafood and choice steaks done in a simple but tasty manner are their strong points.

Garden fresh salad is available both for lunch and dinner. Fresh salmon, steamer clams, oysters, grilled halibut and sautéed prawns are some of the favorite dinners. Breakfasts are served with always pleasant service. Omelettes are a specialty.

Open: every day.
8 a.m. till 10 p.m. Sun. thru Thurs. Till 11 p.m. Fri. & Sat.

NEW YORK WHISKEY STEAK

1 ten oz. New York cut steak   ½ cup whiskey
½ cup mushrooms   ½ cup brown sauce
¼ cup chopped onions   ¼ cup heavy cream
¼ cup salad oil

Heat frying pan and add oil. Brown steak on both sides.
Add mushrooms, onions. Sauté 3 minutes. Add whiskey and flame.
Add brown sauce and simmer for 3 minutes. Add cream.
Serve on a hot plate.

Brown sauce
Boil beef bones with some fat for 4 to 6 hours, then let cool in refrigerator. Skim fat off the top. Bring stock to boil and thicken with roux.

Roux
Melt ½ cup butter, then stir in 1 cup flour. Boil for 2 to 3 minutes. Let stand.

COLD RICE SALAD

6 cups rice   ½ cup diced onions
8 ounces cream cheese   ½ cup diced celery
6 ounces bay shrimp   ½ cup green pepper
1 cup frozen peas   3 cups mayonnaise
4 hard boiled eggs, chopped   4 tablespoons mustard

Cook rice and allow to cool. Soften cream cheese and combine with mayonnaise and mustard.
Stir in other ingredients, mix well and serve.

The central portion of the Polynesian rises over 2 storys in height giving the whole restaurant a majestic feeling, and the use of Northwest cedar is warm and friendly.

Try the macadamia nut muffins with your breakfast. The dinner menu has a good selection of seafood, steaks, chicken and pasta. P.S. The macadamia nut pie is exceptional!

The Polynesian Restaurant is located in front of the Polynesian Resort condominium. It's a full-service resort with 70 units, pool, spa and conference rooms. Many of the rooms have small decks that overlook the Pacific Ocean.

Open: breakfast 7 a.m. till 2 p.m., lunch 11:30 - 2 p.m., dinner 5 - 9 p.m.
Dinner till 10 p.m. on Fri. and Sat.

BROCCOLI & CAULIFLOWER SOUFFLÉ

1 head cauliflower, steamed, drained, chopped
1 head broccoli   "   "   "
½ cup crushed crackers
1 medium onion, chopped
2 eggs, beaten

½ cup mayonnaise
1½ cups thick white sauce
          with mushrooms *
salt and pepper to taste

Pre-heat oven to 350°.

Mix together all ingredients except cheese and pour into 13" x 9" baking dish. (If mixture appears to be too soupy, add ½ cup more of crushed crackers.)

Top with mild cheese. Bake in oven at 350° F. for 30 – 40 minutes.
          *(1 can cream of mushroom soup may be substituted for sauce.)

RASPBERRY BAVARIAN PIE

Pastry crust

2 cubes butter or margarine
½ cup sugar

2 egg yolks
$\frac{2}{3}$ teaspoon salt

Mix the above together. Add $\frac{2}{3}$ cup ground almonds. Add 2 cups all purpose flour. Add enough flour so mixture is not sticky.

Spread into two 10" "Pamed" or greased pie tins. Bake 10 to 12 minutes at 400° F. or until brown around edges.

Filling

(Makes enough for one pie.)
3 cups Cool Whip
1½ cups drained raspberries
3 egg whites
1¼ cups sugar

3 tablespoons lemon juice
½ tablespoon vanilla
1 tablespoon almond extract
¼ teaspoon salt

Beat egg whites till stiff peaks form. Mix all other ingredients (except Cool Whip) in blender. Now combine the blended ingredients, the egg whites and Cool Whip and stir together carefully. Pour into baked pie shell and put into freezer. Let set at least 3 hours before serving.

Arthur Lawrence is the driving force that makes this restaurant a culinary delight. Many extra little touches that add up to a memorable experience......sizzling mushroom appetizers, outstanding soups, salads and entrees that are as pleasing to behold as they are a pleasure to eat!

It is obvious that Arthur enjoys his work, and he has imparted this love to many of the students that he employs (in peak seasons as many as 15 students).

Besides the restaurant, Arthur is president of the Westport Chamber of Commerce. Wife, Susan, teaches school and also helps at "Arthur's".

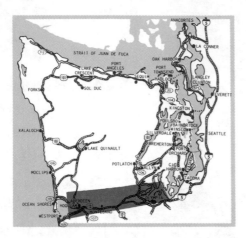

Wing your way down the excellent route 8 from Aberdeen to Olympia and though the road's a pleasure, giving a microcosm of so many elements of Washington, you miss the flavour of the little farming and logging towns on either side. Worth a turn-off (the Greyhound bus route, of course, gives this) to see, for instance, the fine courthouse building of Montesano (its dome an ice cream cone dipped in coconut, sparkling for all to see).

There's such a cosy down-home feel to Elma that couples often choose it as home base when one works in Aberdeen, the other in exactly the opposite direction: Olympia. Thurston County Fairgrounds are just off the route, where you can catch horse-racing, and further down near Olympia you can buy oysters and lovely pottery and fresh baked three grain bread on Mud Bay Road, just one minute off route 8.

All along, farms and meadows, the incongruous nuclear towers of Satsop, unused and farcical, looming over a world of calm sheep and frisky horses. Red-stained barns are brightened with masses of springtime daffodils at Satsop where the nursery draws many gardeners off the highway to shop.

Hoquiam, behind you, has charms like a little ferry to Westport twice a day, like a woodburning fire in the library, and like a marvel of 1920's extravagance in the Mediterranean-style 7th Street Theatre, now, alas, seldom used. Worth driving up the hill near St. Joseph's Hospital for an overview of Aberdeen's harbor, and for a close sight of the handsome big houses round you on that hill...a revelation to those who normally whiz through the flat town and find it charmless. They wonder, as might you, where all the people are and the answer is that, killingly for downtown, Aberdeen has two thriving malls....one with a triple cinema.

Olympia has a fine mall as well (the Bon, Frederick and Nelson, etc.) though it's rather a secret (not signposted from route 8). You've driven through gorgeous Black Hills country, then navigated the tricky swirl towards the city (invariably construction work going on), and you're in a pretty grassy square, edged by handsome Governor's House Hotel, the bus station, and a very good bookshop. Capitol building overlooking the lake brings, of course, life and gossip to this town, and you'll overhear eager lobbiers and go-ahead young politicians at every other table in the town's good eateries.

SL

SECTION **3**

HOQUIAM: Levee Street Restaurant
ABERDEEN: Misty's
MONTESANO: Cornucopia
OLYMPIA: Arnold's, Ben Moore's, Gardner's, La Petite Maison,
Olympic Oyster House, Seven Gables

HAP'S CLAM CHOWDER

¼ pound bacon, chopped
3 medium onions, chopped
3 medium celery, chopped
small amount flour
1 48 oz. can chopped clams
    with juice

1 medium bay leaf
1 pinch Italian seasoning
½ teaspoon garlic salt
4-5 medium potatoes, diced
2 tablespoons heavy cream or
    evaporated milk

Fry bacon till it starts to brown, then drain off the grease into another pan and cook onions and celery in same pan till transparent. Add enough flour to celery and onions to absorb all bacon fat and make a smooth paste.

In a large pot, put a 48 oz. can of chopped clams with juice, bring to a good boil. To this, add the following:

1 medium bay leaf, 1 pinch of Italian seasoning, ½ teaspoon garlic salt, 4 or 5 medium diced potatoes, 1 teaspoon m.s.g., salt and pepper to taste.

Add bacon and cook potatoes till half done. Add enough stock to onions and celery to make a smooth paste about like a medium gravy and add to pot. Continue to cook till potatoes are done. Cook on a low heat, being careful not to let stick to bottom.

As you dish up, add to bowl approximately 2 tablespoons heavy cream or evaporated milk.

SPAGHETTI SAUCE

1 pound ground round
1 cup chopped onions
½ cup green pepper
2 cloves garlic
1 pound tomatoes
1 pound tomato sauce
1 small tomato paste

4 ounce can mushrooms, drained
¼ cup parsley
1½ teaspoons Italian seasoning
1 teaspoon salt
1 teaspoon sugar
¼ teaspoon pepper

Chop parsley and mushrooms. Put all ingredients in pan, cover and simmer 1 hour. Uncover and continue to simmer 20 to 30 minutes or until thick. Stir occasionally.   Serves 6.

The Levee Street Restaurant, located on the bank of the Hoquiam River, is one of the most picturesque in the area.... with a tugboat usually tied up just outside the large scenic windows.... and a view of the bridge connecting Hoquiam and Aberdeen.

The restaurant was once a run-down building housing an old store. It's been remodeled a couple of times to the pleasingly decorated place it is today.

Roy Ann Taylor, the proprietor, has many tempting dishes.... try the bouillabaisse or one of her other seafood dishes.

She states that she is now catering (by special request) for receptions, wedding dinners, champagne brunches and business lunches.

By "Miss T".....

The endless hours I devote to the perfection of foods in Misty's kitchen are seldom questioned, as cooking has become my creative and emotional outlet.

As I was understandably nervous about leaping from employee to employer 3½ years ago, it has taken some maturing to sort out the real significance of all my impressions. A strange but satisfying balance ensued as I hoped that if I approached this task with enough integrity and passion, others would share in an appetite for my personal culinary whims.

Perseverance prevails as plentiful food and exciting people go together at Misty's. 48 imported ales, 4 micro-brews, selective varietal wines from Washington and versatile blended and mixed collections performed with champagne and wine. Espresso, caravali and local herb teas.

Festive, flexible and inspirational dining. "Cooking is like love... it should be entered into with abandon or not at all."

I believe that soup making is one of the most gratifying experiences of all in the vast spectrum of culinary activities. Tender stirring and simmering cannot help but bring forth the loving and nurturing instinct of every soup maker, but it is the finished product that contains the power to assuage the parched palate or soul in truly magical ways.

POTATO LEEK SOUP IN BREAD BOWLS

2 large potatoes, peeled & finely diced
2 large leeks, thinly sliced
4 cups chicken broth, preferably homemade
½ teaspoon salt
¼ teaspoon freshly ground black pepper
¼ cup heavy whipping cream
⅛ teaspoon grated nutmeg

Bread bowls

4 round, unsliced loaves of bread
2 cloves garlic, crushed
4 teaspoons olive oil
4 tablespoons grated parmesan cheese
chopped parsley

In a large pot, combine potatoes, leeks, chicken broth, salt and pepper. Over high heat, heat to boiling. Reduce heat to low, cover and simmer for 15 minutes. Meanwhile make Bread bowls.

Bread bowls: With a small sharp knife, cut into loaf, leaving ¾ inch edge. Hollow out center, reserving leftover bread for croutons. Rub inside with garlic. Brush with olive oil and sprinkle with cheese.
Place hollowed-out loaves and bread "lids" on a cookie sheet and bake in a 350° oven for 15 minutes or until cheese melts.

When the soup has simmered, use a sieve to strain soup into another pan. Place solids in blender or food processor until smooth, return to soup in pan. Stir in heavy cream and nutmeg. Heat through.

Spoon hot soup into bread bowls and top with chopped parsley.

Makes 4 servings.

"We owe much to the fruitful meditation of
our sages, but a sane view of life is,
after all, elaborated mainly in the kitchen."
Joseph Conrad

Misty's Restaurant, located in downtown Aberdeen, is well-patronized by Aberdeen's own, but it is happily discovered by the traveler as well.

"Miss T", Tracy Walthall, had many interesting comments, so instead of the expected 2 recipes, you'll find some of her thoughts printed on the other page.

Open: Monday through Saturday. Closed Sunday.
Lunch from 11 a.m. Dinner from 5 p.m.

APPLE MUFFIN

3½ cups flour
2 cups sugar
1 teaspoon salt
1 teaspoon cinnamon

1 teaspoon vanilla
¾ cup chopped walnuts
3 cups chopped apples *
1½ cups oil

Mix together the flour, sugar, salt and cinnamon. Then add vanilla and chopped walnuts. Stir in the chopped apples and oil.

Heat oven to 350°. Oil muffin tins and fill half full. Bake for 20-25 min.

*Granny Smith apples are preferred.

ORIENTAL CHICKEN SALAD

9 quarts water
3 tablespoons salt
16 oz. oriental noodles

Boil water with salt. Add noodles. Cook 7 min. (until soft) Rinse in cold water. Drain. Pour marinade over and toss.

1½ large red peppers
   cut into 2" strips
6 lg. green onions (including
   tops) cut into 1" strips
6 lg. carrots sliced in food
   processor*
2 cups diced chicken
1½ cups snow peas or
   frozen peas
½ cup toasted sesame seeds

Blanch the carrots for a few minutes.

Add to noodles...sprinkle sesame seeds on top and serve.

MARINADE

¾ cup oil
¾ cup white rice vinegar
8 tablespoons soy sauce
2 teaspoons sugar
1 tablespoon dry mustard

2 teaspoons salt
2 teaspoons peanut butter
1½ teaspoons sesame oil
1½ teaspoons ground ginger
pinch ground pepper

mix in
food processor

Serve room temperature.

The Cornucopia
is located in Montesano -
the oldest settlement in Grays Harbor Co.

The restaurant is housed in the old telephone office building, built in 1915. It is one of a kind in Montesano for the walls are of brick - 24" thick and covered with stucco on the outside. It has in the past housed the telephone company, a judge, 2 doctors, a liquor store, county offices - and now Cornucopia, over-looking the attractive Fleet Park.

Margaret Downey and staff are there to tempt you with new tastes in food and make your luncheon an enjoyable experience - homemade breads enhance their sandwiches.

Open: Monday thru Saturday 11 a.m. till 4 p.m.
Phone: 249-4618.

BREASTS OF CHICKEN RASPBERRY

1 chicken breast (8 oz.)
½ teaspoon garlic
2 ounces butter
1 ounce raspberries
    (fresh or frozen)

2 ounces white wine
2 ounces whipping cream
salt and pepper to taste

Melt butter in sauté pan or large frying pan. Dredge chicken in flour and brown. Add garlic, wine and cream. Bring to a boil, then let simmer from 5 to 10 minutes or until sauce thickens. Add raspberries and salt and pepper to taste.

SEAFOOD FETTUCCINE

1 ounce crab meat
1 ounce shrimp meat
1 ounce scallops
2 ounces snapper
4 ounces shredded parmesan cheese
1 cup whipping cream
½ teaspoon garlic
1 ounce butter
2½ cups cooked noodles

Melt butter in a large sauté pan or frying pan. Add all seafood and sauté for approximately 3 minutes. Add garlic, cream, parmesan cheese and noodles. Simmer until thickened. Add salt and pepper to taste.   2 servings

Arnold's Restaurant, located in one of the most pleasant dining rooms in Olympia, offers both American and continental cuisine.... the candle light and linen make a special atmosphere for your dining experience. You should allow time for a leisurely dinner, as all of their dishes are prepared to order.

Especially thoughtful is their menu offering both normal and light-sized portions. There are selections of beef, chicken, veal and seafood, as well as entrée salads and pasta dishes.... and make their own special sauces. There is full lounge service Monday through Saturday.

Breakfast and lunch are cheerful in the greenhouse setting.

GARDNER'S SALMON (for two)

2 six ounce filets of fresh salmon 1" thick (skin off)
1 cup fish stock
¼ cup dry white wine
1 lime wedge
½ teaspoon chopped fresh basil
½ teaspoon chopped fresh tarragon
16 to 20 red or green seedless grapes
½ teaspoon Pernod or Anisette
Optional: 1 teaspoon leeks, 1 tablespoon thinly sliced fennel root.

Put all of the above (except salmon and grapes) in a shallow pan. Simmer two minutes, add salmon and simmer five to eight minutes with lid on. Take salmon out and put on warm plate. Return sauce to stove, remove lime wedge, season with salt and fresh pepper, lemon juice, ½ teaspoon Pernod or Anisette. Add grapes and heat thoroughly. Pour over salmon, serve with lemon or lime wedge.

CHOCOLATE ESPRESSO CHEESECAKE WITH KAHLUA SAUCE

Crust

Mix 1 cup graham cracker crumbs, 1 cup finely chopped almonds, 2 tablespoons sugar, 2 tablespoons flour. Add 1 ounce melted semi-sweet chocolate and 3 to 4 ounces melted butter. Mix well, pat into 10" spring form pan and bake at 350° for ten minutes (or until golden brown). Cool.

Filling

Mix 2 pounds of cream cheese and 1 cup sour cream, both at room temperature. Add 3 tablespoons flour, 1 cup sugar, ½ cup instant espresso powder, 6 ounces melted semi-sweet chocolate and 1 teaspoon vanilla. Add five eggs, one at a time. Pour into crust, bake at 300° for one hour, turn off oven and leave cheesecake in for an additional 15 minutes. Remove and cool overnight.

Kahlua Sauce

Mix one cup milk, ⅓ cup sugar, 3 egg yolks, 1 tablespoon flour. Cook over low heat until thick, remove from heat and add 1 ounce semi-sweet chocolate, ½ teaspoon vanilla, ¼ cup Kahlua. Pour over individual cheesecake slices.

Gardner's, located in the exciting Percival Landing-Farmer's Market area, specializes in Northern Italian and seafood dishes, but owner-chef Gene Gardner and cooks Lorie Rains and Leon Longan provide a variety of "from scratch" items, with a selection that should please everyone. Desserts are a specialty.

Their proximity to the water makes them ideal for boaters and visitors; the relaxed atmosphere makes you feel welcome regardless of dress. (No smoking.)

Open daily from 5 p.m. till 9 p.m.

MICHAEL MURPHY'S OYSTERS AL PESTO

Pesto Sauce (enough to last awhile)

1 cup olive oil
2 cups fresh basil*
   finely chopped

2 cloves garlic, minced
½ cup chopped pine nuts or
   toasted almonds

Pureé in food processor the basil, garlic and nuts. Add olive oil immediately in a steady stream. Let set at least 1 hour before using.

Oyster base for one person

8 small oysters (a bit
   larger than yearlings)
⅓ bunch small-leaf fresh spinach

1 cup cooked fettuccine
fresh grated parmesan cheese

Wash and separate the spinach leaves. Lay out oysters in lightly oiled cooking pan over low heat and sauté a few minutes, turning frequently, until they are puffed and slightly browned. While they are cooking, add ⅓ cup of pesto sauce and spinach. Stir and turn until the spinach is thoroughly wilted and coated with sauce.

Toss fettuccine with 2 tablespoons of pesto sauce, remove to a plate, cover with oyster mixture and top with grated cheese.

* (or use ½ to 1 cup dried basil)

OYSTERS MATRICIANA

8 medium small Pacific oysters
2 strips of bacon, diced
2 tablespoons chopped onion
1 tablespoon chopped green pepper
¼ cup sliced mushrooms

1 fresh tomato, cut into
   half inch cubes
dash of catsup
black pepper to taste

Sauté diced bacon, add onion, green pepper and mushrooms. Cook two minutes over medium heat; add oysters. Cook three or four minutes, add tomato, black pepper and catsup. Cook two minutes. Serve with pasta.

Old flavor and new flavor meet at popular Ben Moore's. The building dates from 1906 when Fourth Avenue was a dirt track, and the cafe at Moore's sports a photograph of workmen cobblestoning the street in 1908.

Ben Moore founded the cafe+bar from a barber shop, tavern and Chinese cafe. in 1948; and just one year later, an earthquake tumbled part of the next door building through Ben's roof.

Michael Murphy, who bought Moore's in 1984, is one of the wave of cooks who uses only organic vegetables. His seafood is fresh, meat choice and lean and cheeses (Tillamook cheddar, for instance.) He's proud of his star in "Northwest Best Places."

NORTHWEST SAUTÉ

12 ounces oysters (combination of Pacific and Pioneer)
6 ounces veg.(combination zucchini, mushroom, onion **Julienne**)
4 tablespoons butter
½ cup white wine
2 pinches garlic powder
2 pinches paprika
combination of 7 herbs & spices
salt and white pepper to taste

In a sauté pan, melt butter, then add vegetables and sauté till onion is transparent. Add wine and seasonings. Immediately add oysters and cook until done. Do not overcook oysters. (If Pacifics are very large, poach first and cut in half before adding to vegetables).

Serves 2.

J.J. Brenner
supervising an
opening line.
1910

PEPPER PAN ROAST

1 pint of shucked Olympia oysters
2 tablespoons of butter
3 to 4 tablespoons cocktail sauce
pepper to taste
toast points

Put the well rinsed oysters into a sauté pan with butter, cocktail sauce and pepper. Simmer. Then stir gently. Serve on toast points.   Serves 2.

The Olympia Oyster House is located in the old original culling house of Olympia Oyster Company dating back to the mid 19th Century. As far back as 1859 oysters were sent to San Francisco, where gourmets paid $20 per plate for them. These oysters are only grown in the cool waters of lower Puget Sound, between Shelton and Olympia.

In 1925 the original owners started a small seafood bar in the southeast corner of the building. In 1948 this evolved into a large scale operation; and after 2 or 3 additions it has become the noteworthy restaurant that you will find now. Needless to say, they know how to prepare excellent oyster dishes, as well as many other items.

Oct.-April: Mon.-Fri. 11 a.m.-9 p.m.   Sat.-Sun. noon-10 p.m.
May-Sept.: Mon.-Fri. 11 a.m.-10 p.m.   Sat.-Sun. noon-11 p.m.

STUFFED POULET

2½ pound poulet (young chicken)
cooked wild rice
hazel nuts

medium size orange
½ dozen morel mushrooms
salt and pepper
butter

Poach in water, ½ cup cooked wild rice, 4 tablespoons coarsely chopped hazel nuts and ½ dozen morel mushrooms. Add the zest of one medium size orange. (If dried morels are used, reconstitute overnite in either water or cream sherry.)

Rub the poulet cavity with salt, pepper and ½ tablespoon whole butter. Stuff poulet with the rice, nuts and morels and bake in preheated 375° oven uncovered for 40 minutes.

SMOKED SALMON SALAD

2 pounds boneless quality smoked salmon
½ cup chopped parsley
⅔ cup mayonnaise
½ cup sour cream
2 small thinly sliced shallots
2 tablespoons capers
squeeze fresh lemon juice

Combine all of the above and stuff into an avocado or a tomato. Serve on a bed of lettuce.

Another way: Poach an artichoke, take out insides and stuff with the salmon mixture and serve on lettuce bed.

The chefs at La Petite Maison believe that the immigrants to the Northwest were instantly charmed by the fresh and seasonal foods that are so bountiful to the Pacific Northwest ....existing on the staples of the land. This generation carries on...and to this end, La Petite Maison has 2 acres of new European flat and Olympic oysters maturing. Their nearby farm produces herbs, lettuce, raspberries and strawberries.

They have a fine reputation for serving outstanding dishes with care given to all aspects.

GORGEOUS PRAWN SAUTÉ

2 cloves mashed garlic
½ cup diagonally sliced celery
¼ cup diced red onions
¼ cup unsalted cashews
¼ cup sliced dried apricots

¼ cup grated gorgonzola cheese
dash of: apricot nectar
          fresh lemon juice
          dry white wine
24 peeled and deveined prawns

Sauté vegies and nuts in peanut oil until just tender (don't make them limp). Add prawns and cook until they turn opaque. Add the dashes of liquids and cheese. Cook just long enough to melt gorgonzola cheese and coat the ingredients. Serve at once.   Yield: 4 servings.

SUNDAY BRUNCH SCONES

Sift together

3½ cups flour
⅛ cup sugar
2⅛ tablespoons baking powder
2 teaspoons salt

Cut into dry mix

2½ sticks unsalted butter

Add to above

⅔ cup milk
2 eggs (beaten)
juice from one lemon & grated rind

Knead dough 20 – 30 times. Round into 4 balls. Shape into flat rounds ¼" thick. Cut into 8 pieces.

Brush with egg and bake on ungreased sheet at 425° for 10 to 13 minutes.

Yield: 30 scones.

Enjoy traditional home-cooking served in an historic 1892 house with porch inviting a view of Mt. Rainier and Olympia's harbor. The parlor of Seven Gables is an intimate bar with a sunset deck. Wedding receptions and parties unwind in the hillside garden.

Open: Tuesday through Saturday, Dinner at 5 p.m.
Sunday, Champagne brunch 9:30 till 2 p.m.

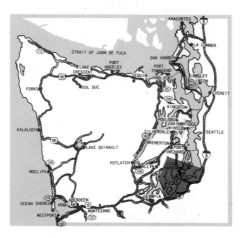

But where's the <u>town</u>? Visitors to Tacoma are initially dismayed to see it stretching somewhat forlornly along the harborfront, with many a building boarded up or collapsing.

But there are surprises: super meals at the city's many waterfront restaurants and at the very good one picturesquely above it all. A charming little art museum smack downtown, gorgeous rambling Point Defiance park out on the spot where the ferry to Vashon sails out.

Fascinating Historical Museum, very central, with good book and gift shop. Lots of patchwork neighborhoods amongst those hilly streets, many tree-profuse and always the thriving choc-full Mall out on I-5 which has virtually killed downtown Tacoma shopping.

Lovely casserole mixture of types over on rural Vashon Island: old traditional farming people, some Brooks Bros. families, the last of the 60's hippies, some excellent professional crafts creators, famous makes, too, of all-fruit jams, chutneys. The peace and quiet crowd on Vashon welcomes the mainland set in July for merry strawberry festival...parade of youngsters, a band, lots of shortcake booths, a good crafts fair in grassy dell that's a shopper's delight.

More chic, considerably more affluent in mood, is Tacoma's dream dormitory (fast exploding with new homes), Gig Harbor, just over the Narrows Bridge. A lovely wander among small and good boutiques (don't miss the famous quilt collection), a bobbing marina, always, wherever you stroll, view of the Sound and sailing boats. Shop for pleasant clothes and crafts as you work up an appetite for the good restaurant meals round the harbor.

SL

SECTION 4

TACOMA: Antique Sandwich Company, Hogan's, Lessie's, Raintree, Stanley and Seafort's
GIG HARBOR: W. B. Scotts, Neville's Shoreline
VASHON: Sound Food

LEMON-HONEY CHEESECAKE

This recipe is for a 10 inch spring-form pan or similar pan.

Crust

2 cups graham cracker crumbs $\frac{3}{4}$ cube melted butter
2 tablespoons honey

Mix the ingredients and press into pan, up the sides with a straight edged glass – do it while the mixture is still warm.

Filling

1$\frac{1}{2}$ pounds cream cheese $\frac{2}{3}$ cup honey
$\frac{1}{2}$ squeezed lemon   3 whole eggs
1 tablespoon pure vanilla $\frac{1}{3}$ cup non-instant non-fat powdered milk
                                                  (available in health food stores)

Cream cheese should be at room temperature. Beat cream cheese, lemon and vanilla thoroughly, so there are no lumps. Mix honey into above, then mix in eggs. Gradually mix milk powder into the whole filling and look for a texture that is creamy.
Bake at 300° for 40 minutes in preheated oven. Have pan of water in oven to create moisture.

Topping

$\frac{1}{2}$ pint sour cream   1 tablespoon honey
$\frac{1}{2}$ squeezed lemon $\frac{1}{2}$ teaspoon pure vanilla

Thoroughly mix while cheesecake is baking – after removing from oven carefully spatula the topping on to the hot cheesecake. Let it bake on as the cheesecake cools. Refrigerate several hours and serve.

GINGERBREAD

3$\frac{1}{2}$ cups whole wheat pastry flour   2 teaspoons ground ginger
1 tablespoon baking powder $\frac{3}{4}$ cup vegetable oil
1 teaspoon baking soda   1$\frac{1}{2}$ cups black strap molasses
1 teaspoon cloves   3 eggs
2 teaspoons powdered mustard   1$\frac{1}{2}$ cups hot water
2 teaspoons cinnamon

Sift all the dry ingredients into a mixing bowl and add the oil, molasses, hot water and egg yolks. Mix. Beat the egg whites separately. Add wet to dry ingredients. Fold in egg whites. Put into greased flat baking pan and cook in preheated 350° oven for 40-45 minutes.

Bake at 300° in preheated oven for 40 minutes. Have pan of water in oven to create moisture.

The Antique Sandwich Company has been a center for good food and good music for almost 15 years. The emphasis is upon nutritional whole foods in sandwiches, home-made soups, quiches, whole wheat desserts, fresh ciders, juices. Breakfast items such as waffles or cinnamon rolls have been well-appreciated in Tacoma.

The response is not only to the food, but to the community feeling that derives from their concerts and open mikes, benefit events and from an atmosphere that encourages people to sit, relax and converse. (Open mike is on Tuesday.)

Open: Mon.- Sat. at 7 a.m. Close Mon., Wed., Thurs., Sat. at 8 p.m. Sunday 8:30 till 7 p.m.   Close Tues. at 10 p.m. Fri. at 9 p.m.

HALIBUT RAINIER

4 (6 ounce) halibut steaks or filets
½ cup butter (melted)
½ cup lemon juice

½ cup sour cream
½ cup cheddar cheese
½ cup bay shrimp or shrimp meat

1. Preheat oven 350°. Place halibut in shallow baking dish.
2. Combine melted butter and lemon juice and pour over fish.
3. Bake for 10-15 minutes or until fish is cooked and flakes easily. Do not over-cook, or it will be dry.
4. Remove from oven.
5. Top each steak with sour cream, cheddar cheese and shrimp.
6. Broil just until cheese melts.

Note: Try topping on other white fish.   Serves 4.

SPINACH SALAD DRESSING

½ jar (8 oz. size) dijon mustard
1 onion, chopped fine
1½ teaspoons Worcestershire sauce
1½ tablespoons lemon juice

2 teaspoons salt
dash Tabasco
1½ cups red wine vinegar
3 cups salad oil

Mix all ingredients together well. It's ready.

Hogan's Bay Company invites you in by
way of a covered walkway..... a help in a down pour! In nice
weather you'll find the crowd on the deck enjoying the magnificent view of
Puget Sound. It's an olde English-inn style building perched atop rugged
pilings over the waters.
The menu includes many favorites, with a special note about the prime
rib, seafood fettuccine and Halibut Rainier (see recipe on opposite page).

Lunch Mon.- Fri. 11:30 till 2:30 p.m.   Sat. 11:30 till 3:30 p.m.
Dinner Mon.- Fri. 5 till 10 p.m.   Sat. 5 till 11 p.m.   Sun. 4 till 9 p.m.
Sunday brunch 10:00 a.m. till 2:00 p.m.

OLD FASHIONED BISCUITS

2 cups all-purpose flour
3 teaspoons baking powder
1 teaspoon salt
4 tablespoons shortening

About $\frac{2}{3}$ cup milk or $\frac{1}{3}$ cup evaporated milk and $\frac{1}{3}$ cup water

Cut shortening into sifted dry ingredients until consistency of coarse corn meal. Add enough milk, while stirring, to make a soft dough that can be easily handled. Knead on floured board, then roll or pat til $\frac{1}{2}$ to 1" thick. Use cutter of desired size, place on greased or oiled baking pan. Bake in 450° for 12 to 15 minutes. Serve hot.

BEEF STROGANOFF

$\frac{1}{4}$ cup all-purpose flour
$\frac{1}{2}$ teaspoon salt
1 pound good quality beef, cut in $\frac{1}{4}$ inch wide strips
$\frac{1}{4}$ cup butter
$\frac{1}{2}$ cup chopped onion
1 cup thinly sliced mushrooms
1 clove garlic

1 tablespoon tomato paste
$1\frac{1}{4}$ cups beef stock or 1 can condensed beef broth
1 cup sour cream (can be left out for dieters)

1. Combine flour and salt and dredge meat with this mixture.
2. Heat skillet, add $\frac{1}{2}$ the butter; when melted, add meat and brown quickly on both sides. Add mushrooms, onion and garlic. Cook 3 to 4 minutes, till onion is barely tender.
3. Remove meat and mushrooms from skillet and add remaining butter to the pan drippings. When melted, blend in remaining flour with whisk. Add tomato paste, and slowly pour in the meat stock. Cook while stirring, till mixture thickens.
4. Return meat and mushrooms, stir in sour cream and heat briefly.

Lessie helped her parents for years in their restaurant, and now her sons help at Lessie's Southern Kitchen.... after school or during vacations. This is a down home casual place, and the tables might all be full, but it's worth the wait. The catfish are flown in from Louisiana, grits are served with some of the meals (unless you prefer potatoes). She does a super job on liver and onions, but whatever you try, save room for her home made sweet potato pie or bread pudding!

Open every day from 7 a.m. till 7 p.m.

RAŽNJIĆI (Raz-Nee-Chee)

Yugoslavian shish-kabob. Lamb, pork, vegetables on skewers.
10 servings. Great for the outdoor BBQ. Can be made a day in advance.

1 pound lamb, deboned and cleaned	onions
1 pound pork butt, excess fat trimmed	green pepper
olive oil	red pepper
garlic	zucchini
salt and pepper	tomato
whole rosemary	mushrooms*

1. Marinate lamb in olive oil, clove of garlic, whole rosemary, salt, fresh pepper for at least 4 hours.
2. Marinate pork in olive oil, garlic, salt and pepper at least 4 hours.
3. On 12" skewers place 2 parts pork to 1 part lamb, alternating with vegetables to your liking (suggestions above).
4. Charboil and serve with rice or pasta.
* If you prefer your medium to well done, make skewers of meat and vegetables separately to assure that vegetables are not well-done.

AMARETTO CHEESE CAKE

1 pound cream cheese	4 teaspoons almond extract
¾ cup sugar	4 tablespoons Amaretto
3 cups sour cream	graham cracker crust
3 eggs	9½" spring form pan
2 teaspoons vanilla extract	

1. Coat sides and bottom of pan. Make crust and refrigerate.
2. Cream together cream cheese and sugar.
3. Add sour cream, eggs, extracts and Amaretto. Mix.
4. Pour mixture into pan and bake for 2 hours at 300°.
5. Let cool to room temperature then refrigerate overnight.

16 servings

The Raintree Restaurant offers fine continental cuisine 365 days a year. The fresh seafood, choice beef, chicken and pastas are complemented by cajun, continental and European styles of cooking. Their dedication to quality and service stems from the team work of American trained chef Joseph Moine and Yugoslavian born owner John Vukas.

Joseph is well-versed in a variety of cooking styles, while John supplies many ideas for the European specialties. Quality, variety and service make this a dining experience.

Open Monday thru Saturday 11:30 a.m. till 9 p.m.
Sunday 3 p.m. till 9 p.m.

ROAST PRIME RIB OF BEEF

Roasting Rock-Salt Method with Fresh Horseradish:

beef prime rib
Lawry's Seasoning Salt

coarse ground pepper
rock salt

Cover bottom of roasting pan with food-grade rock salt. Place prime rib, bone-side down, on salt. Season rib with 1 tablespoon seasoning salt and 1 teaspoon pepper for each 4 pounds of roast.

Cover rib completely with more rock salt and place in 210° oven for 9 to 10 hours. Roast until internal temperature measures 125°. Remove from oven and let rest for 30 minutes to set the juices and make roast easier to carve. When ready to serve, remove all salt from rib and carve.

Fresh Horseradish

Scrub fresh horseradish root with a brush under running water. Freeze root to help control aroma when peeling. Peel root, then grate in small shreds. Place shredded horseradish in a colander and pour boiling water over it; drain. Mix 3 cups shredded horse-radish with ½ cup cider vinegar, 1 tablespoon sugar and ½ teaspoon salt. Marinate for 2 hours, then serve with prime rib.

ORIGINAL BURNT CREAM

Rich vanilla custard made from fresh eggs and pure cream, with a caramelized, crackling sugar crust.

1 pint whipping cream
4 egg yolks
½ cup granulated sugar
1 tablespoon vanilla extract

Sugar for the topping

4 tablespoons granulated sugar
to 1 teaspoon brown sugar

Preheat oven to 350°. Heat cream over low heat until bubbles form around the edge of pan. Beat egg yolks and sugar together until thick, about 3 minutes. Gradually beat cream into egg yolks. Stir in vanilla and pour into 6 6-oz. custard cups. Place custard cups in baking pan that has about ½ inch water in bottom. Bake until set, about 45 minutes. Remove custard cups from water and refrigerate until chilled. Sprinkle each custard with about 2 teaspoons sugar blend. Place on top rack under broiler and cook until topping is medium brown. Chill before serving.   Makes 6 servings.

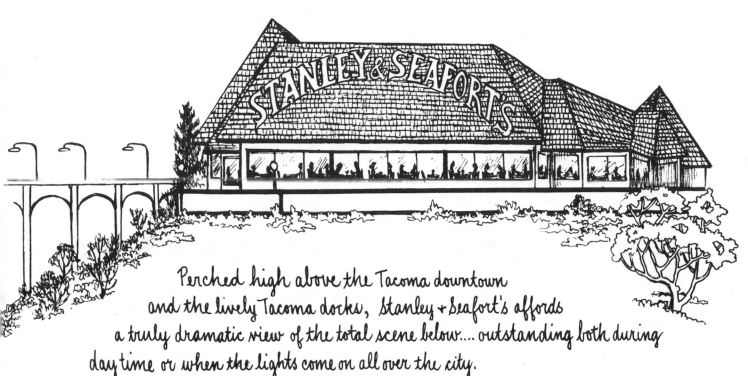

Perched high above the Tacoma downtown and the lively Tacoma docks, Stanley + Seafort's affords a truly dramatic view of the total scene below.... outstanding both during day time or when the lights come on all over the city.

This statement on their menu tells their policy:

"Stanley + Seafort's Steak, Chop and Fish House is, above all, an attitude: One that captures a spirit, combining a sense of community and congeniality with an active and freewheeling atmosphere. We have dedicated our efforts to recalling that spirit in our restaurant."

Other items worth noting: They serve Certified Nebraska Select ™ beef, custom-selected, 28-day locker-aged, corn-fed.... exceeds USDA choice-grade standards. Hand cut premium grade filet fresh fish. All dressings and sauces are hand made.

CARROT CAKE

1 teaspoon salt
4 eggs
2 cups grated carrots
1 cup well drained crushed
    pineapple
1 cup oil
2 cups flour
2 cups sugar
1 teaspoon cinnamon
1 teaspoon clove

1 teaspoon nutmeg
2 teaspoons baking powder
2 teaspoons baking soda
1 cup walnuts
8 ounces butter
8 ounces cream cheese
1 teaspoon lemon
1 teaspoon vanilla
1 pound confectioners sugar

Mix carrots, pineapple, eggs, oil, cinnamon, cloves, nutmeg, salt and walnuts. Then add flour, sugar, baking powder, baking soda and mix until well blended.

Pour into two 9" round pans. Bake in preheated oven 350° for approximately 40 minutes. Check with toothpick. Cook until done.

Frosting

Blend butter and cream cheese with lemon and vanilla until smooth. Add sugar and slowly mix until creamy.

Serve as a 2 layer cake or cut and make a 4 layer cake.

FAJITAS

flour tortillas
    (2 per person)
$\frac{1}{2}$ cup safflower oil
$\frac{1}{4}$ cup lime juice
$\frac{1}{4}$ cup red wine vinegar
1 clove garlic, minced
$\frac{1}{2}$ teaspoon salt

1 cup orange juice
$\frac{1}{4}$ teaspoon black pepper
$1\frac{1}{2}$ pounds skirt or flank steak
1 large onion, sliced
salsa
guacamole

1. Combine all juices and oil, garlic and seasonings; mix well.
2. Place steak in juice and leave 24 to 36 hours in refrigerator.
3. Before serving, grill onions or sauté with $\frac{1}{2}$ teaspoon oil in skillet until brown.
4. Drain meat from marinade, grill until medium rare...cut meat into strips.
5. Serve with onions on a sizzling griddle (meat will cook slightly). Serve with flour tortillas, salsa and guacamole.

W.B. Scotts occupies the lower floor of what once was the "Peninsula Hotel." Built in 1923 by the Gilich family, the hotel served as a meeting and gathering place for Gig Harbor folk and was occasionally used as a courthouse. The ferry landing was located across the street on Harborview Drive.

W.B. Scott's space was the home of the Peninsula Cafe which provided hotel guests and local residents with food and beverages. Rumor has it that one of the former tenants made moonshine in the cellar under the hotel!

There are banquet facilities available.

Open 7 days a week for breakfast, lunch and dinner.

HALIBUT DIJONNAISE

4 halibut filets
8 ounces baby shrimp
4 ounces artichoke hearts
1 tablespoon dijonnaise sauce
8 slices havarti cheese

Dijonnaise sauce

½ cup mayonnaise
2 teaspoons country style
    dijon mustard
salt and pepper to taste
dash of lemon juice

Place halibut filets in baking pan. Place 2 ounces shrimp, 1 ounce artichoke hearts, 1 tablespoon dijonnaise sauce and top with havarti cheese on each filet. Bake in preheated 350° oven for 20 minutes or until fish is firm.   Serves 4.

AVOCADO MELT

2 ripe avocados
4 ounces crab meat
4 ounces baby shrimp
4 ounces grated cheddar cheese (reserve
   ½ to top avocados)

2 ounces grated onions
2 ounces chopped celery
mayonnaise- enough to moisten
   crab mixture
salt and pepper to taste

Mix all ingredients together except the avocados. Peel, halve and pit the avocados. Fill with the seafood mixture, top with remaining cheese and bake 15 to 20 minutes at 350°. Serve with hot rolls and tossed salad.

Serves 4.

Neville's Shoreline is terraced down towards the water so that you have different postcard views of the harbor and Mount Rainier in the distance. There's always activity to entertain you as you dine..... pleasure and fishing boats, even an occasional row boat. (It's as interesting after dark when all of the lights come on.)

Entertainment is periodically offered for dinner shows. The food is of top quality, pleasingly presented. As expected, there is a good selection of fresh seafoods, as well as a wide variety of other tempting entrees.

Mon.-Sat. lunch 11 a.m.-3 p.m.   Dinner 5 - 10 p.m.
Sun. brunch 9:30 a.m.- 2:30 p.m.   Dinner 4 - 9 p.m.
Lounge 11 a.m. till midnight

ALU GOBI CURRY with Lemon Rice, Lentil Dal and Banana Rayta

*An Indian adventure of tastes! Potato and cauliflower curry served
with flowery lemon rice, lentil and onion dal, and cooling banana rayta.
The more condiments the better, so try pappadams or chapatti flatbreads,
chutneys, nuts, seeds, dried fruits.....*

CURRY

1/4 cup clarified butter (ghee)
1 tablespoon ginger, minced
1 tablespoon garlic, minced
1 tablespoon cumin
1 teaspoon turmeric
2 teaspoons mustard seed
2 teaspoons garam masala*
2 teaspoons salt

1/4 teaspoon cayenne
1 onion, chopped
3 carrots, sliced
2 potatoes, diced
1 cauliflower, flowerettes
3 tomatoes, chopped
1/3 cup vegetable stock
1/3 cup cider

2 teaspoons lemon juice
3 tablespoons orange juice
(concentrate)
1/4 cup chili sauce (or barbecue sauce)
1/2 cup béchamel sauce
1/2 pound peas, frozen

Sauté ginger, garlic, cumin, turmeric, mustard seed, garam masala, salt and cayenne in ghee for 2 to 3 minutes. Add onion and sauté until limp. Add carrots and potatoes and sauté 5 minutes. Add liquids (vegetable stock, cider, lemon juice, orange juice, chili sauce, bechamel sauce) to vegetables, stirring to blend well. Bring to simmer, cover and cook 30 minutes or until vegetables are tender. Add frozen peas and cook 5 minutes more, until heated through.

*Garam masala – a roasted blend of spices for curries (makes 1/4 cup)

1 cinnamon stick
1 tablespoon cardamom seeds
2 tablespoons cloves

2 tablespoons cumin seed
1 tablespoon coriander seed
2 tablespoons pepper corns, black

Roast at 200° for 30 minutes, stirring once or twice. Let cool. Crush cinnamon sticks in a towel with rolling pin or mallet. Grind spices to a powder. Cover tightly to store.

LEMON RICE

1/4 cup ghee
1/2 onion, chopped fine
2 cups white basmatti rice
1/2 teaspoon turmeric

1/2 teaspoon cardamon powder
peel of 1/2 lemon, grated
3 cups water
1/2 teaspoon salt

Sauté until limp the ghee and onion. Wash rice well until water runs clear. Drain. Add to onions and sauté 3 to 5 minutes until shiny. Add spices and sauté briefly. Then add hot water with salt and bring to boil, cover, reduce heat and simmer 30 minutes.

LENTIL DAL

Bring lentils to boil in water with spices. Cover partially and simmer 30 minutes until soft, and liquid is reduced. Meanwhile sauté onion and cumin seed in ghee, stir into lentils when done and simmer 5 minutes more. Adjust seasonings.

BANANA RAYTA

3 tablespoons ghee
1 tablespoon mustard seeds

3/4 cup shredded coconut
3 cups yogurt

1/4 **teaspoon** coriander
2 bananas, mashed

Briefly sauté mustard seeds in ghee. Add coconut and remove from heat. Add yogurt. Add spices and mashed bananas. Mix well.

Located on Vashon Island, the Sound Food Restaurant is a delightful place with large windows that face a well-tended garden where in late spring a corner wisteria blooms profusely. The old wooden floors give warmth, and there is a relaxing feeling that prevails throughout the restaurant. Their own ovens turn out an incredible array of freshly-baked goods: sprouted wheat and seven-grain breads, cinnamon rolls, cheese Danish, cookies, muffins and mouth-watering pies.

The weekend brunches on Saturdays and Sundays are very popular with islanders and visitors alike.

Open: Mon., Wed., Thurs., Fri. for lunch.   Wed.- Mon. for dinner.
Sat. & Sun. for brunch.

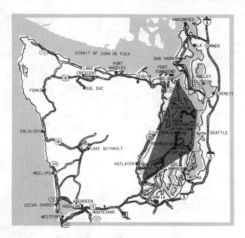

Take highway 101 that wends its way through lazy countryside until near the Skokomish Indian Reservation, then watch for the Bremerton signs (on highway 106 turnoff). This highway 106 passes through Union where you will see, from the side of the road, the old Dalby waterwheel built in 1922, that is now heavily moss-covered and frequently sketched and photographed. If you are having hunger pangs by the time you reach the little village of Allyn, it is worth finding the Bellagambas restaurant, far off the beaten path. All of this part of 106 is on the tip of the hook ending of the Hood Canal. Port

Orchard is close to Bremerton, but far different in atmosphere. There are antique malls, shops, and a couple of good spots to eat and a view across to Bremerton. A 15 minute foot-ferry links Port Orchard and Bremerton and goes right by the Navy's celebrated mothball fleet. Until 1990 the USS Nimitz warship will be moored here. In Bremerton the Naval Museum (half a block from the ferry terminal) tells of ship building history back to bowspit and sailing days. There is also a foot-ferry between Seattle and Bremerton that runs weekdays and the ride is only 35 minutes rather than the 2 hours on the large ferry.

Silverdale has taken a lot of business from Bremerton and boasts of many shops. Northward to Poulsbo, a town that whole-heartedly is Norwegian... in its decor, heritage and the many annual events, such as the Viking Fest, Poulsbo Art Fest, and Octoberfest...to mention a few. Locals call it "Little Norway".

To reach Bainbridge Island from Poulsbo heading south means crossing the Agate Pass Bridge on highway 305. The ferry to Seattle lands at Winslow, an interesting little town... so spend some time here.

One of the many fun experiences for this general area is the West Coast Oyster Shucking Championship and Washington State Seafood Festival that is held the first week in October each year.

BW

SECTION **5**

ALLYN: Bellagambas
PORT ORCHARD: Neon Sky, Spice of Life, Tweten's Lighthouse
BREMERTON: The Boat Shed, Pat's Cookie Jar
SILVERDALE: Granny's Pantry, Silverdale Inn (Mariner)
POULSBO: Henry's, Poulsbo Creek
BAINBRIDGE ISLAND: Pleasant Beach Grill
WINSLOW: Saltwater Cafe
KINGSTON: Pacific Sojourn

CHOCOLATE, CHOCOLATE CHIP CHEESECAKE

8" springform, buttered

3   8 oz. packages cream cheese
4 eggs
1 cup sugar
4 ounces semi-sweet chocolate
7 tablespoons butter

1 cup sour cream
¾ cup chocolate chips
1½ teaspoons vanilla
pinch of salt

Crust

1½ cups crushed chocolate cookie wafers
sprinkle of sugar and walnuts
¼ cup melted butter

Mix together and press into sides and bottom of springform pan.
Preheat oven to 325°.

Filling

In electric mixer, cream the cheese with eggs and sugar until smooth.
Melt chocolate and butter together and add to the cheese mixture with
sour cream, vanilla, salt, chocolate chips. Blend well and bake in oven
for 1 hour and 15 minutes, or until top crackles. Let cool at room
temperature, then chill overnight.

DUNGENESS CRAB CASSEROLE

4 slices bacon, diced
2 tablespoons clarified butter
2 tablespoons green onions, sliced
   (use tops only)
1 teaspoon diced shallots
¼ teaspoon garlic, minced

4 ounces sliced mushrooms
2 tablespoons white wine
6 to 7 ounces Dungeness crab
1 cup shredded mozzarella and
   cheddar cheese
½ cup heavy cream

Prepare and have all ingredients on hand. Preheat oven to 425°. Over
medium heat, fry bacon until brown and fat is rendered. Remove bacon
and put on paper towel. Drain fat. Over high heat, add butter, onion,
shallots, garlic and pepper until garlic is golden brown (about 1 min.).

Add mushrooms and bacon and cook 30 seconds more. Deglaze with wine
and add crab and cream. Cook until hot throughout. Remove from heat
and place in 6-ounce casserole dishes, adding just enough of the cream
to keep moist. Cover with ½ inch layer of cheese and bake until cheeses
are melted and bubbling around the edges. Serve immediately with rice
and vegetable.

96

Bellagambas Unique Dining is well off Highway 3 that passes through Allyn, so watch for either Bellagambas' sign down town or the sign for the Lakeland Golf and Country Club. (It's like discovering a quality pearl in an oyster!)

Owners Dave and Gail DiRito state "We believe in quality food ... fresh meats, milk-fed veal, fresh seafood, real cream, butter and cheese. All of the soups, sauces, dressings and desserts are made here."

Bellagambas' is located on the lower floor of the Lakeland Country Club House.... there's a great view of a charming pond with ducks swimming about.

Open: Tues.-Thurs. lunch noon till 4 p.m., dinner 4 till 9 p.m. Fri.-Sat. dinner till 9:30 p.m. Sunday open noon till 8 p.m.

KALBI SALMON

2 pounds salmon filets (cut in 4 pieces)
Marinade:

1 cup soy sauce
½ cup sugar
½ cup water
2 teaspoons minced
   fresh garlic

1½ teaspoons sesame oil
1 teaspoon fresh grated ginger
1 teaspoon honey

Prepare marinade and then add salmon filets. Cover and refrigerate for 1½ hours. Bake in 400° oven for 6 minutes. Garnish with toasted sesame seeds and thinly sliced green onion. Serves 4.

CRAB AND CHEESE STUFFED PRAWNS

Stuffing:

9 ounces crab meat, minced fine
3 green onions, minced fine
3 teaspoons mayonnaise
¾ cup fine bread crumbs
3 teaspoons minced shallots

1½ teaspoons minced garlic
¾ cup fresh grated parmesan cheese
juice of 1 lemon
24 green headless prawns   21/25 size

Shuck prawns, except for tail section on end of prawn. Devein, butterfly and flatten prawn meat. Lay flat on a cellophane covered tray. Freeze until firm. Put about 1 teaspoon of filling on flat part of frozen prawn. Pack it around the prawn, so that it is rounded. Freeze stuffed prawn again until filling is firm.

Heat deep fat fryer to 350°. Dip in beer batter and fry for 4 minutes. May be served with hollandaise sauce.

Beer batter

¾ cup flour
2 eggs, separated
1½ teaspoons salt

2 tablespoons salad oil
¾ cup beer at room temperature
freshly ground black pepper

Beer batter procedure

Place flour in mixing bowl and add egg yolks, salt, oil, beer and a grind or two of fresh pepper. Stir the batter clockwise with a whisk until thoroughly mixed. Cover the bowl with plastic wrap and allow to rest for anywhere from 2 to 24 hours.

Stir the batter well, In a separate bowl, beat egg whites with a whisk until stiff, but not dry. Fold into batter. You are ready to go !

Wonderful dining is taken to great heights at Neon Sky.
Located at the Bremerton National Airport. Take advantage of the great view through huge greenhouse windows as planes take-off and land. Your tastebuds will soar with a wide selection of entrees and specialties.....fresh daily seafood, meats (featuring prime rib) and unique poultry creations. There's an excellent selection for the Sunday Brunch including omelette bar.... bottomless glasses of champagne are also available.

Lunch: Mon.-Sat. 11 a.m. till 3 p.m.   Sun. Brunch 9:30 till 2:30 p.m.
Dinner: Mon.- Thurs. 5 till 9 p.m.   Fri. & Sat. 5 till 10 p.m.
        Sunday 4 till 9 p.m.

CLAM CHOWDER

1 onion, chopped
5 medium potatoes, diced
1 clove garlic, minced
1 carrot, chopped
1 stalk celery, chopped
2 tablespoons green pepper,
    finely chopped

¼ cup flour
2 tablespoons butter
1 large can chopped clams
    (reserve liquid)
1 quart whole milk
1 quart boiling water

Sauté onion and garlic in butter until golden. Alternate layers of clams and vegetables, dredging each with flour, salt and pepper. Slowly stir in boiling water, mixing lightly. Simmer till potatoes are soft. Add milk and reserved clam broth. Add a pinch of basil and tarragon.

ZESTY MEXICAN SOUP

1 can tomato paste, 15 ounces
1 can tomato sauce, 15 ounces
4 fresh tomatoes, peeled & chopped
½ cup frozen corn
1 medium zucchini, diced
1 clove garlic, minced
½ onion, chopped fine
1 package (8 oz.) cream cheese, diced
1 cup chicken broth
1 cup diced, cooked chicken breast
2 tablespoons butter
2 tablespoons cumin
1 teaspoon seasoning salt
½ teaspoon pepper

Sauté onion and garlic in butter. Add remaining ingredients except cream cheese. Simmer about 20 minutes. Float cream cheese on top and serve.

The Spice of Life Espresso Bar and Gallery is located one block from the beautiful Port Orchard waterfront. A mixture of arts and culinary delights culminates in an atmosphere of relish and culture.... walls and shelves display many forms of art media... a room features an artist of the month. Homemade soups and other delectables are complemented by delicious espresso or other beverages. A variety of gourmet coffees, teas, spices and cordials is available by the pound, ounce or cup.

Open   Monday – Saturday 10 a.m. till 6 p.m.
Sunday noon till 5 p.m.

TWETEN'S LIGHTHOUSE TOASTED SEASONED BAGELS

Slice onion bagels ¼" thick and lay flat on baking pan. Drizzle with melted garlic butter and bake at 350° approximately 12 minutes or until golden brown. Serve with cream cheese spread.

Cream cheese spread

1 pound cream cheese
2 tablespoons sour cream
1 teaspoon fresh ground horseradish
2 tablespoon bacon bits
pinch black pepper

Beat all ingredients together in blender.

LIGHTHOUSE CHEESECAKE

Crust 10" Spring form

2 cups graham crackers
½ cup butter
½ cup sugar

Filling

2 pounds cream cheese
1 cup sugar
3 eggs
1 tablespoon sour cream
1 teaspoon pure vanilla

Bake 325° for 1 hour and 5 minutes, or until toothpick comes out clean. Remove from oven and let cool 10 minutes.

Topping

2 cups sour cream
¼ cup sugar
1 teaspoon pure vanilla

Spread topping evenly and bake 4 minutes. Sprinkle with reserved crumbs.

The Lighthouse Restaurant offers a spectacular view of Sinclair Inlet and the Bremerton shipyards. The interiors are handsomely decorated with teak and brass.

Chef John Salmons specializes in fresh Pacific northwest seafood, with entrees including steamed or sautéed lobster, oysters Rockefeller or try the seafood selection of the day... also prime rib, pepper steak, chicken Oscar.

Portions are more than ample, but save room for the homemade cheese cake....a different flavor daily.

Enjoy a bountiful Sunday brunch as the buffet chefs cook omelettes and flambé crepes to order.

Mon.-Sat. Lunch 11 a.m.- 4 p.m. Sun.-Thurs. Dinner 4-10 p.m. Fri. till 10.
Sun. Brunch 9:30 a.m.- 2 p.m.   Lunch 2-4 p.m.   Dinner 4-10 p.m.

BOATSHED CHILI

1 pound lean ground beef
1 cup chopped onions
1 cup chopped green pepper
1 cup chopped celery
1 clove garlic, minced
2 tablespoons olive oil
1 tablespoon beef base in
  1 cup hot water

1 16 oz. can tomatoes, cut up
1 16 oz. can dark red kidney beans
1 16 oz. can chili beans
1 16 oz. can tomato sauce
1 teaspoon cumin
2 teaspoons chili powder
1 teaspoon dried basil

In large stock pot cook ground beef, put in strainer to drain off fat, set aside.

In same pot sauté vegetables in olive oil until soft.

Add ground beef and rest of ingredients. Bring to boil, reduce heat and simmer uncovered for about 2 hours, stirring frequently.

Makes 6 to 8 servings.

SEAFOOD PASTA

$\frac{1}{4}$ cup butter or margarine
$\frac{1}{2}$ cup thinly sliced green onions
  (including tops)
3 tablespoons all-purpose flour
1 cup chicken broth
$\frac{1}{2}$ cup bottled clam juice
$\frac{1}{4}$ cup dry white wine
$\frac{1}{4}$ cup whipping cream
$\frac{1}{4}$ teaspoon oregano leaves

$\frac{1}{2}$ cup grated parmesan or
  shredded swiss cheese
1 clove garlic, minced or pressed
$\frac{1}{4}$ pound mushrooms, sliced
4 ounces rotelle
  (boiling salt water)
$\frac{3}{4}$ pound small, cooked shrimp
6 ounces scallops
1 6 ounce can sea clams

Stir together chicken stock, clam juice, wine, whipping cream, oregano and onions in medium sauce pot; cook on medium heat, stirring until it comes to a boil. Remove from heat and make a roux, add to above and add cheese. Stir until blended, then set aside.

In large skillet on medium high heat, sauté mushrooms and garlic in butter for 3 to 4 minutes. Add to cream mixture.

Sauté scallops briefly, add to mixture along with shrimp and clams. Stir mixture well. Pour into an 8" x 13" glass baking dish.

Bake 350° oven for 20-25 minutes.

The Boatshed
was originally a marina with
boat building and storage facilities. It was converted in
the early 70's into a restaurant. The restaurant is built on pilings
with a large deck for use in the summer.

Seafood, meat, fowl, pasta, soup, salad, sandwiches are available all of
the time. A full bar complements the restaurant.

Open: lunch & dinner Mon. thru Thurs. 11 a.m. till 1 a.m.
dinner only on Sun. 3 p.m. till 10 p.m.

CHICKEN MULLIGATAWNY

2 quarts chicken stock
3 cups diced tomatoes
2 cups celery
1 diced green apple
1 diced green pepper
¼ cup onion, diced
½ pound deboned chicken

½ cup rice
2 whole cloves
2 teaspoons curry powder
⅛ teaspoon pepper
¼ cup butter
¼ cup flour
2 cups milk

Simmer all ingredients except rice and roux until tender. Then add rice and simmer until done. Separately make a roux of butter, flour and milk by melting butter, stirring in flour and gradually stirring in milk. Cook until thick. Then add to soup.   Makes approx. 1 gallon.

BLUEBERRY BUCKLE

1½ cups sugar
½ cup margarine
2 eggs
1 cup milk
⎫ A

4 cups flour
1½ teaspoons baking powder
1 teaspoon salt
⎫ B

Cream well the ingredients from A, then add ingredients from B. Fold in 4 cups blueberries, pour in 9 x 13" pan (lightly greased). Sprinkle on the topping and bake for 50 minutes at 350°.

Topping

1 cup sugar
½ cup margarine
⅔ cup flour
1 teaspoon cinnamon

Cut in with pastry blender.

Pat Ekoes of Pat's Cookie Jar Restaurant and Bakery said that she tries to offer home-style meals that are "out of the ordinary". Some of her specialties are home made breads, old-fashioned desserts, cinnamon rolls and pies. The cars line up early in front of Pat's, because she starts serving at 6 a.m. and is well-known for the one-skillet breakfast (as well as a selection of eye-openers). There are always home-made soup at lunch time and dinner specials such as chicken and dumplings.

Open: Monday through Saturday 6 a.m. till 9:30 p.m.
       Sunday from 6 a.m. till 7:30 p.m.

BROCCOLI AND CHEDDAR SOUP

6 cups chopped broccoli
10 cups pork broth <u>or</u>
    3 tbsp. ham soup base *
1 cup dry non-dairy creamer
2 cups grated cheese
1 cup flour
salt and pepper to taste

Cover broccoli with pork broth and cook until tender. Mix flour and non-dairy creamer with 2 cups water. Add to broccoli. Add cheese. Salt and pepper to taste.

Garnish with cheese. For creamier soup, add more non-dairy creamer.

*Use 10 cups of water.

HONEY BREAD

7 to 8 cups all purpose flour
1 cup non-fat dry milk powder
3 pkgs. active dry yeast
1 tablespoon salt

3 cups warm water
⅓ cup soft butter or margarine
⅓ cup honey

Place 2 cups flour, milk powder, yeast and salt in large mixing bowl. Pour in water and beat one minute using electric mixer. Add butter and honey. Beat 1 minute longer. Gradually add enough flour to make soft dough. Beat well, using a heavy duty electric mixer or wooden spoon. Turn out on a lightly floured board.

Knead 5 to 10 minutes or till smooth and satiny. Place in greased bowl. Lightly butter top of dough. Cover with towel. Let rise in a warm place until doubled in size (about 1½ hours).

Punch dough down. Turn out on lightly floured board. Knead gently for 1 or 2 minutes to remove air bubbles. Divide into 3 pieces. Shape into loaves. Place in 3 greased 9 x 5" loaf pans. Cover with clean towel. Let rise in warm place till doubled in size (about 35-40 minutes).

Bake in 375° oven 40-45 minutes or till golden brown, and loaves sound hollow when thumped.   Makes 3 loaves.

Granny's Pantry began in '83 as a partnership, but Mary Berg has been the guiding force since '85. She recently spent a week in Amish country in Pennsylvania gathering Amish recipes, then experimented and worked up her own versions. Now, every other Thursday is "Amish night" for dinner.

Then featured alternating Thursdays is German, Italian, Mexican or Irish night.

This is a friendly, homey place. Some customers say "It's like being in Grandma's kitchen."

Try to save room for a piece of peanut butter pie or raisin sour cream pie! Mary has shipped her pies to Hawaii, Florida, Washington D.C. and California. A smoke-free restaurant.

Open: daily from 9 a.m., except on Sat. from noon. Breakfast till 11 a.m.
Mon. and Sat. closing at 3 p.m. Open till 8 p.m. other days.

CRAB LEG AMBASSADOR

1 tablespoon butter
1 tablespoon chopped fresh shallots
½ teaspoon thyme
1 egg yolk

6 Dungeness crab legs
½ cup cognac
½ cup heavy cream
fresh chopped parsley

Sauté on medium heat the butter, shallots, thyme and meat from the crab legs. Cook 3 minutes. Remove from pan and deglaze with cognac. Add cream. Reheat all ingredients, adding 1 egg yolk. Stir then remove from fire. Serve on toast. Sprinkle with fresh chopped parsley.

BROCCOLI SOUFFLÉ

3-4 stalks broccoli
5 tablespoons flour
5 eggs, separated
salt

white pepper (to taste)
dash of nutmeg
1 cup heavy cream

Preheat oven to 350°. Cook broccoli in salt water approximately 6 minutes, drain and put through meat grinder. (Need about 1 pound pulp) Put in food processor.

Melt butter in saucepan and stir in the flour, using wire whisk. Add cream, stirring until mixture is thick and smooth.

Remove sauce from heat and beat in egg yolks, one at a time, stirring rapidly. Add salt, pepper and nutmeg.

Beat egg whites until stiff. Stir in half the whites, using whisk. Fold in remaining whites, using rubber spatula. Do not overmix. Pour into a soufflé dish, bake 35-45 minutes, or until soufflé is puffed and browned.

Note: other vegetables that may be used for this soufflé are:
cauliflower, carrots and zucchini.

The Mariner Restaurant is located on the main floor of "Silverdale on the Bay" ..... literally built on the beach. Unusual angles allow a sweeping panorama of Puget Sound. The wood construction used throughout lends a warm feeling. This Pacific Northwest resort and convention hotel can handle groups of from 5 to 500.

Shape up in the glassed-in heated pool, the sauna or jacuzzi; on the lighted tennis, pickleball or shuffleboard courts; in the exercise and weight room.

The Mariner Restaurant features fine NorthWest cuisine, and while dining, you'll enjoy seaside views by day and romantic candlelit ambiance by night.

Open Mon.- Fri. at 6 a.m.   Sat.-Sun. at 7 a.m.
Close Sun.- Thurs. at 10 p.m.   Fri.-Sat. at 11 p.m.

phone
698-1000

HENRY'S PEANUT BUTTER CREAM CHEESE PIE

Pecan Pie Shell

1½ cups toasted and finely chopped pecans
½ cup sugar
¼ teaspoon cinnamon
¼ cup melted clarified butter

Mix all ingredients. Use fingers to press mixture onto bottom and sides of 10" pie tin. Chill in freezer while preparing filling.

Peanut Butter Cream Cheese Filling

1 cup Jif brand creamy peanut butter
8 ounces cream cheese - softened
2 tablespoons melted clarified butter
1 cup powdered sugar
1 cup heavy cream whipped with ¼ cup powdered sugar
     and 1 tablespoon vanilla

With electric mixer set on high, beat together peanut butter, cream cheese, butter and sugar until fluffy. Beat the 1 cup cream with ¼ cup powdered sugar and vanilla and fold whipped cream into the peanut butter mixture. Spoon into chilled pie crust, cover with plastic wrap and refrigerate till firm (about 2 hours).

Spread fudge topping over top of pie. Decorate with more whipped cream around edge of pie. Chill and serve with your favorite coffee. Sooo good!

HENRY'S BREADED OYSTERS SUPREME

The secret to breading oysters so that the breading does not come off when pan or deep frying.

1 pint fresh oysters (size determined by oyster lover)
2 large grade A eggs
1 cup milk
2 cups cracker crumbs

Rinse oysters with cold water and pat dry. Beat eggs well in mixing bowl, add milk and blend.

Dip oysters in milk and egg mixture. Dip in cracker crumbs, covering thoroughly, pat between hands to be sure crumbs stick and oyster is well coated. Place on waxed paper on a flat pan (a cookie sheet works well). Place in freezer for a minimum of 30 minutes. If you wish, you may put them in some type of freezer container and freeze for up to 2 months. The breading does not fall off when done in this manner. When ready to complete, sauté for 2 to 3 minutes (depending on size) and serve with your favorite coleslaw.

As you enter Henry's Family Restaurant, you are in a unique Scandinavian atmosphere....truly outstanding hand-crafted quilts are framed and on display. The use of tile, painted murals and antiques completes the look that Jerry and Gini Henry have created in this family-owned restaurant since May 13, 1975. The Henrys are known world-wide for their cream and fruit pies. Large breakfasts are served, and lunch and dinners feature Swedish roll-ups, home made soups, clam chowder, home-baked turkey, family-style chicken, steaks and seafood. There are cocktails, Washington wines and non-alcoholic beverages available.

Open: every day from 7 a.m. till 9 p.m.

OYSTERS POULSBO CREEK

oysters, small
brandy
garlic butter (see recipe)

parmesan cheese, grated
asiago cheese, grated

Wash and shuck oysters as needed. Combine cheeses and set aside.
Place oysters back into shells and place in baking pan on rock salt to hold
shells steady. Sprinkle each oyster with $\frac{3}{4}$ teaspoon brandy and top with 1
teaspoon garlic butter and $1\frac{1}{2}$ teaspoons grated cheese mixture.

Bake in preheated 400° oven until cheese is melted and oysters are poached
in garlic butter and brandy, or about 8-10 minutes. Serve as appetizer or
entrée.

Garlic Butter

1 pound butter, softened
$\frac{1}{2}$ cup green onion, chopped
$1\frac{1}{2}$ teaspoons white pepper
2 tablespoons lemon juice

2 dashes Worcestershire sauce
2 dashes Tabasco sauce
$\frac{1}{8}$ cup chopped garlic

Mix all ingredients until well-blended.

CHICKEN JACK DANIELS

$\frac{1}{4}$ gallon chicken stock
4 ounces Jack Daniels whiskey
$\frac{1}{2}$ cup garlic, chopped
2 red peppers, roasted
2 green peppers, roasted

$\frac{1}{4}$ cup black and green olives,
    chopped
$\frac{1}{2}$ pound red onions, thinly sliced
butter, softened
chicken breasts, skinned & boned

Bring chicken stock, whiskey and garlic to boil. Reduce by 25 percent. Cut
peppers into Julienne strips. Add remaining ingredients, except chicken and
butter. Simmer for 45-60 minutes.

For single serving, brown chicken breast in butter. Turn and add $\frac{1}{2}$ cup of
stock. When chicken breast is cooked, remove from pan and reduce stock by
one-half. Remove from heat and add softened butter chunks and blend well
to make thickened liaison. Pour over chicken breast and serve hot.

The rustic and art deco setting at the Poulsbo Creek Chop and Fish House lends itself to a relaxing atmosphere for lunch and dinner. It is a classic white linen steakhouse complemented with fresh seafoods. They are striving to serve an exciting cuisine using highest quality fresh ingredients. The Bistro Bar features an array of libations and potables including Kemper beer on tap.

Mon.-Sat. Lunch 11:30 a.m.-2:30 p.m.   Dinner 4:30 - 10 p.m.
Sunday champagne buffet brunch 10 a.m. - 2 p.m.   Dinner 4 - 9 p.m.

MEDITTERANEAN BOUILLABAISE

½ cup olive oil
2 tablespoons fresh minced garlic
3 cups diced carrots
3 cups diced celery
3 cups diced onions
1 cup white wine
3 cups clam juice
2 cans whole tomatoes
2 tablespoons tomato paste
1 teaspoon dry basil*
1 teaspoon dry oregano*
1 teaspoon dry thyme*
*if fresh, use twice as much

3 bay leaves
2 teaspoons fennel seeds
cayenne pepper to taste
a pinch of saffron (optional)
1 pound clams
1 pound mussels (debearded)
½ pound prawns
½ pound sea scallops
½ pound fish (such as snapper or
    cod, cut into pieces)
fresh chopped parsley
4 crayfish

Heat olive oil in a heavy pot over medium heat. Add garlic, carrots, onions and celery and cook for a few minutes, stirring constantly. Add wine, bring to a boil and let it reduce to half. Add clam juice, tomatoes, tomato paste and all spices. Simmer for 10 to 15 minutes. Add all seafood and cook until clams and mussels start opening. Keep warm.   Serves four.

BAKED OYSTERS PLEASANT BEACH

20 oysters, such as Quilcene, Shoalwater
    (allow 5 oysters per person)
½ pound soft butter
2 tablespoons fresh minced garlic
1 tablespoon fresh minced shallots

2 sprigs green onions (green part only) diced
½ cup brandy
fresh grated parmesan cheese
chopped fresh parsley
2 pounds rock salt

Heat oven to 425°. Shuck oysters and put aside, saving the bottom part of oyster shell. Wash each shell very well. Heat one tablespoon of butter and sauté garlic and shallots for a few minutes. Deglaze pan with brandy and reduce to half (be extremely careful when you pour brandy into pan. It tends to ignite). Transfer garlic and shallots onto a plate and let cool.

Mix butter, garlic, shallots and green onions very well. Spoon 1 teaspoon garlic butter into each shell. Place 1 shucked oyster on top of butter, cover with parmesan cheese. Put rock salt on baking pan, place oysters on top. Bake for 15 to 20 minutes until cheese is melted and golden brown. Garnish with parsley. Serve immediately.   Serves 4.

Pleasant Beach Restaurant, an elegant restaurant nestled in the woods of the southwest corner of Bainbridge Island, is easily accessible from the Winslow Ferry.

The building, a 2-story English Tudor mansion, was formerly a family home. Many islanders have fond memories of times past spent at recitals and social gatherings there.

It was converted into a fine restaurant and has maintained its elegant character..... wood paneled library lounge, marble fireplace, hardwood floors. Window dining in both the lounge and main dining room affords a view of Rich Passage & passing ferries. The owner/chef uses fresh herbs, vegetables, dry-aged meat and excellent sea food.

Open: for dinner and cocktails starting at 5 p.m. nightly.
Sunday brunch served 10 a.m. till 2 p.m.

BLACKENED SALMON

Blackened salmon seasoning mix

6½ tablespoons paprika
1½ tablespoons onion salt
½ tablespoon garlic powder
2½ tablespoons dried thyme
2½ tablespoons dried oregano

3 tablespoons dried dill
1 tablespoon ground white pepper
1 tablespoon ground black pepper
2 teaspoons cayenne pepper
1 teaspoon salt

Put all ingredients for blackened salmon seasoning in a large container and mix well.

4 8 ounce salmon filets, bias cut
4 tablespoons butter
4 tablespoons minced fresh parsley

Place salmon in container and toss well until filets are coated with mix. Press filets into mix to insure proper coating. Set salmon aside, save remaining seasoning mix for another use. (Use on meats, poultry, seafood.)

Heat heavy gauge 8" sauté pan on high heat till very hot. Preheat oven to 150°. Put 2 filets in pan (no oil). Pan should smoke at first. Turn heat down, sear salmon for 4-5 minutes. Turn salmon over, cook till medium (firm to touch). Remove filets from pan and keep warm in oven.

Repeat procedure with remaining salmon. Spoon ½ tablespoon butter on each piece of salmon. When melted, sprinkle with fresh parsley. Serves 4.

HONEY MUSTARD DRESSING

3 tablespoons white vinegar
3 tablespoons water
1 tablespoon Kosher or sea salt
1 tablespoon fresh minced parsley
1½ teaspoons garlic powder
1 teaspoon fresh minced oregano
   (or ½ tsp. dried oregano)
1 teaspoon fresh minced basil
   (or ½ tsp. dried basil)

1 teaspoon dried mustard
2 tablespoons dijon style mustard
2 teaspoons red wine
pinch dried thyme
3½ tablespoons honey
1 cup sour cream
¾ cup salad oil

Combine first 12 ingredients in large stainless steel mixing bowl, let stand for 10 to 15 minutes. Add sour cream to the bowl, whisk ingredients together. Drizzle in salad oil, whisking constantly.   Makes one quart.

The Saltwater Cafe is well worth a trip to Bainbridge Island....
it's located on the waterfront overlooking the beautiful
Eagle Harbor, and the cafe is just 5 blocks from the
Winslow Ferry.

They feature seafood, pasta, salads, delicious steaks
and specialty Cajun dishes. On nice days dine outdoors on the
patio. Northwest beers, wines and cocktails are available.

Open seven days a week 11:30 a.m. till 9:30 p.m.

PACIFIC LASAGNE

This is a meatless lasagne, but Eric and Gina say
it is just as "yummy" as traditional lasagne.

3 cups tomato sauce
8 large, flat wholewheat lasagne noodles
1 bunch fresh spinach (wash, dry, chop small)
1 cup cottage cheese (or ricotta cheese)
6 artichoke hearts (fresh, canned or marinated) chopped in small pieces
4 ounces raw milk cheddar or regular cheddar cheese grated
2 to 4 cloves garlic, crushed
4 ounces mozzarella, grated

Cook noodles in boiling, salted water until tender. Rinse and drain.
Oil 8" x 8" baking dish. Place ⅓ of noodles flat, but overlapping on
bottom of dish. Mix cottage cheese, artichoke hearts, spinach and
garlic together... spread fairly evenly in a layer over the noodles.
Spread tomato sauce in layer over the last layer. Then put layer of
⅓ cheddar and mozzarella mix.
Top with another layer of noodles and repeat until you have three layers
of everything, ending with mozzarella and cheddar on top.
Put into pre-heated 350° oven for 40 minutes and let stand 10 minutes
before cutting.   Serves 4 to 6.

WHEAT-FREE GRANOLA

So many people have wheat allergies
that this recipe should be of some help.

2 cups rolled rye
2 cups rolled oats *
2 cups rolled barley
½ cup sunflower seeds
½ cup honey
¼ cup coconut (natural, unsweetened)
¼ cup pure maple syrup
¼ cup walnuts chopped
¼ cup almonds chopped
3 tablespoons sunflower oil **or**
    butter melted

Mix all ingredients, spread thinly on large baking sheet. Stir frequently
as it slow-bakes about 2 hours. Oven heat 225°. This will give it crunch
without overcooking the ingredients.

* may be purchased at health food store

After talking to Eric and Gina, it is obvious that they are 100% dedicated to serving organic products... from organically grown coffees, Swiss water-processed de-caf, _no_ refined sugar or flour, naturally raised poultry, beef and lamb.

They create their recipes from scratch.

Because most of the produce is purchased from local small farmers who emphasize organic growing methods, the daily specials will vary according to what is available in season.

Open Tuesday thru Sunday 9 a.m. till 9 p.m. (usually).

Definitely don't be in a hurry traveling in this area! From the southernmost part of the picturesque Hood Canal and following 101 northward, you'll want lots of film to capture it all. Start by leaving 101 briefly 12 miles north of Shelton, turn east to Union where the view from Alderbrook has the Hood Canal, a busy boat landing and the snow-capped mountains in the distance.

Soon after the return to highway 101, the road passes through the Skokomish Indian Reservation and hugs the Hood Canal on the east, while skirting the outer edges of the Olympic National Park on the west side of the highway.

This is the ultimate for the fishermen, campers, hikers, nature lovers... so

there are many camping areas - Lake Cushman, Elkhorn, Hamma Hamma. Lena Creek, Seal Rock, Interrorom, Dosewallips ...to mention a few. Fishing includes steelhead, salmon, bottom fishing, crabbing, clamming. The Hood Canal offers scuba diving and boating. For backpackers into Olympic National Park and Forest, one good entrance is from Lake Cushman State Park.

At Quilcene (famous for its oysters) the road forks, but either 101 North or Center Road will take you to historic Port Townsend.

There are knowledgable ship builders here... many come to construct their own.

In May and September many of the beautiful old Victorian homes are opened to the public and are well worth seeing. The oldest festival in town each May brings crowds for the week-long activities for Rhody Week. Near-by Fort Worden has camping facilities and lots more for everyone ...one of the most successful cultural programs in the state, Centrum, with chamber music, writers conferences, plays, jazz, theater performances, classes, seminars, and more. You can arrange to stay in one of the officers' houses while you take courses with Centrum. You probably noted Fort Worden in the film "An Officer and a Gentleman" a few years back.

The Hood Canal joins with the Puget Sound north of Port Ludlow and becomes the Strait of Juan de Fuca as it passes Fort Worden.   BW

SECTION **6**

UNION: Alderbrook Inn
POTLATCH: Canal Side
HADLOCK: Ajax, Old Alcohol Plant, Nancy's
PORT TOWNSEND: Aldrich's, B.Joe's, Bread and Roses,
  Landfall, Lido, Little Red Kettle, Salal, Water St. Deli

JOE'S FRITATA

2 ounces clean Dungeness crab meat
2 ounces scallops
2 ounces peeled, drained small shrimp
8 ounces whipped eggs
1 ounce fresh spinach

2 ounces fresh parmesan
2 ounces sliced oyster
   mushrooms
salt & pepper to taste
dash fresh lemon juice

Toss all ingredients in bowl, as you would a salad. Preheat teflon pan with 1 ounce clarified butter. Brown on both sides and bake till firm in 400° oven (approx. 5 minutes). Top with dollop sour cream and an edible flower.

HALIBUT IN PARCHMENT

6 ounces boneless halibut filet
1 ounce clarified butter
1 ounce Julienne celery
1 ounce Julienne carrot
pinch of leek, sliced thin

salt and fresh ground black
   pepper to taste
white wine
parchment paper

Cut parchment paper to 14" size heart. Place halibut on left of heart. Top with remaining ingredients, fold right side over left, starting at tip of heart, starting at tip – fold or crimp a quarter inch of paper lip. Continue to fold up to top and start back at bottom till paper is sealed around halibut. Bake in 400° for 12 minutes.

The Alderbrook Resort is located on the beautiful Hood Canal, a fjord-like inlet of Puget Sound and framed by the towering snow-capped Olympic Mountains. The restaurant, just above the beach and boat docks, offers a variety of delectable seafood entrees and delightfully prepared house specialties. Their chowders are totally satisfying. The Sunday champagne brunch is an event you don't want to miss!

Dining room open every day from 7 a.m. till 9 p.m., except on Fri. & Sat. closes 10 p.m.   Sunday brunch begins at 9 a.m.

KRAUT SALAD

1 #10 can sauerkraut, well drained
1 cup chopped green peppers
1 cup diced onions
1 small can pimiento, chopped

1 cup vinegar, white
1 cup oil
3 cups sugar

Mix above ingredients, chill and serve.

CLAM PATTIES

1 cup bread crumbs
1 tablespoon chopped onions
1 egg
2 6½ ounce cans minced clams

Drain liquid from clams, reserve. Stir ingredients together and add liquid as needed to be able to form patties.
Fry till golden brown in oiled frying pan.
Good served with lemon wedges and tartar sauce.

You'll wonder
what's happening when
you see the line of cars in
front of the Canal Side Restaurant....
especially Friday night for the all-you-can-
eat seafood buffet and salad bar..... shrimp cocktail,
oysters on the half-shell, oysters fried, geoduc, fresh fish and much more! The
setting is rustic with booths and counter, and rows of tables in the back room....
be sure to bring your appetite, because the servings are generous every day,
and the prices are reasonable.

Open every day from 6:00 a.m. till 10:00 p.m.

BARBECUE RIBS

beef ribs
burgundy wine
soy sauce
Worcestershire sauce
cheddar cheese

Marinate the ribs overnight in burgundy wine, soy sauce, Worcestershire sauce and water in equal parts.

Bake in 375° oven until meat is loose on rib bones. Place ribs on a baking rack and cover with balance of sauce. Top with cheddar cheese.

Bake until cheese is melted.

CRAB AND SHRIMP SAUTÉ

2 ounces celery
2 ounces carrots
2 ounces cauliflower
2 ounces broccoli
2 ounces zucchini
2 ounces yellow onions
2 ounces mushrooms

2 ounces shrimp
2 ounces crab
3 ounces cheddar cheese
dry white wine
garlic purée
seasoning salt

Cut first 7 ingredients into 1" pieces.

Sauté in dry white wine, garlic purée and seasoning salt.

Top with 2 ounces each of crab and shrimp. Then top with 3 ounces of shredded cheddar cheese. Bake in 350° oven for 5 to 6 minutes.

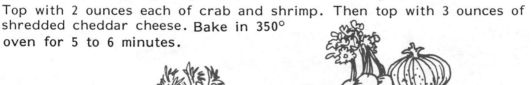

Hadlock's landmark
dining experience — famous for
delectable fresh seafood dishes, flame-broiled
steaks and a one-of-a-kind atmosphere. It's described in
"Northwest Best Places" as "intimate and comfortable.... furnishings
are funky and almost old." Wine and beer are served. There is live
music nightly.

CHICKEN MARSALA

chicken breasts	basil
parmesan cheese	fresh mushrooms
eggs	butter
lemon	olive oil
marsala	parsley

Pound the deboned chicken breasts until very thin.

Dip in whipped egg, then in parmesan cheese. Then refrigerate for two to three hours.

Melt butter and olive oil and sauté chicken until golden brown. Add marsala, lemon juice, mushrooms, basil and parsley, chopped.

SCAMPI

butter	lemon juice
olive oil	green onion, chopped
garlic powder	large shrimp, peel, devein
salt	
dash cayenne	

Preheat oven to 400°.   Use large ovenproof skillet.

Combine the first seven ingredients, melt and mix well. Add the shrimp coated with the butter mixture.

Bake 8 minutes.

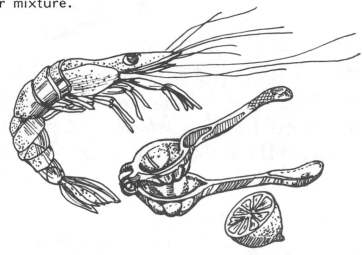

The Old Alcohol Plant really was an alcohol plant from 1911 till 1913. Alcohol, made from sawdust, was shipped to San Francisco until it ran into problems.

Eastern producers and San Francisco distillers didn't like the competition, so the plant began making alcohol from molasses. The Sugar Trust became upset and bought controlling interest only to let the plant close.

The buildings stood vacant most of the next 65 years, when Ray Hansen bought the plant and spent 9 years and $3,000,000 turning it into a hotel and resort.

The Old Alcohol Plant restaurant, adjacent to the resort lobby, gives diners a view of the Port Townsend Bay and offers an elegant menu featuring seafood and steaks.

Located in Hadlock near Indian Island. (14 miles north of Hood Canal Bridge.)

Open every day.   Breakfast 7 till 11 a.m.   Lunch 11:30 till 4 p.m.
Dinner 4 p.m. till 9 p.m., except on Fri. & Sat. until 10 p.m.
Off season: open for breakfast, lunch, dinner. Call for hours.

POLISH POTATO SOUP

5 slices bacon, finely diced
2 cups onions, chopped
1 quart water
5 to 6 cups potatoes, diced
¾ head cabbage, chopped
1 tablespoon seasoning salt
½ teaspoon ham flavoring
½ pound package non-dairy creamer
   (Coffee Mate)

Brown bacon, then add onions. Cook until tender. Add water
and remaining ingredients. The sausage should be cut into
thin circle slices. Cook on medium heat about 30 minutes,
stirring occasionally.

RAISIN CREAM PIE

1 baked 9" pie shell
1 cup granulated sugar
6 tablespoons all-purpose flour
⅛ teaspoon salt
2 cups scalded bottled milk or
   1 cup evaporated milk and
   1 cup water, scalded

3 eggs, separated
1 teaspoon vanilla extract
½ cup raisins
½ teaspoon cinnamon

Combine ½ cup of the sugar, the flour and salt: add the milk while stirring.
Cook in top of double boiler over boiling water for 10 minutes, stirring till
thick. Beat egg yolks with ¼ cup of the sugar, then add hot mixture
gradually while stirring. Cook 5 minutes in double boiler. Cool: then add
vanilla. Stir in cinnamon and raisins.

Pour pie filling in pie shell and bake in 300° for 30 minutes.

Note: If you like meringue, use the remaining egg whites. Beat
them until quite stiff, then add gradually 6 tablespoons of sugar.
Cover the cream filling with the meringue and bake as directed
above. Whipped cream is another choice for topping. Makes 1 9"
pie.

If you're looking for a very casual spot, Nancy's Place is the place... definitely "come as you are". Nancy loves to try new recipes and tends to be adventuresome. The cooks, if in a good mood, will try most anything. One day there was a discussion over who made the biggest butterhorns, so Nancy began making them really large. Now she claims "they are the biggest butterhorns in the Northwest." Breakfast is served all day. The pies are home-made, and they disappear fast! Now in its sixth year.

There is also a full bar and a gift shop at Nancy's.

Open: Mon. thru Fri. 11:30 - 4:30 lunch, 5 - 9 p.m. dinner.
Sat. 4 - 10 p.m. dinner. Sun. 4 - 9 p.m. dinner.

SALLY'S STRAWBERRY TRUFFLE PIE

1 baked 8" pie crust
1 box ripe strawberries
6 ounces chocolate chips
2 tablespoons butter
8 ounces cream cheese

3 tablespoons Grand Marnier
   (orange juice may be
   substituted for this)
¼ cup powdered sugar

Mix chocolate chips, butter, Grand Marnier and cream cheese in saucepan over low heat. Stir until melted, then remove from heat. Stir in the powdered sugar.

Pour filling into pie shell and chill until set. Slice strawberries decoratively over the pie.
                               Serves 6.

TOM'S CHICKEN AND SHRIMP JAMBALAYA

3 bay leaves
1½ teaspoons salt
½ teaspoon cayenne pepper
1 tablespoon dried oregano
½ teaspoon white pepper
½ teaspoon black pepper
¾ teaspoon thyme
2½ tablespoons oil
3 pound chicken, cut up
   (use back and neck for stock)

½ pound smoked sausage, cut into wheels
6 medium prawns, peeled and split
1½ cups onions, chopped
1 cup celery, chopped
¾ cup bell pepper, chopped
4 cloves garlic, chopped fine
½ cup dry white wine
1 can tomatoes, 16 ounces
1½ cups uncooked long grain rice
2 cups chicken stock

Combine first seven ingredients and set aside.

In 4½ qt. dutch oven heat oil to medium, add chicken, brown lightly. Add sausage, stir frequently. After 2 minutes add onion, celery, bell pepper and garlic, continue stirring often, till vegetables are wilted and transparent.

Add spices and wine and stir. Add can of chopped tomatoes with its juice and simmer for 5 minutes.

Add rice, stock and prawns and bring back to simmer, then reduce heat. Cover and simmer until rice is tender, and no liquid remains (about 45 minutes). Salt to taste.
If more heat is desired, add Tabasco.

Sally's
Elegant foods
to delight your palate and please your eye.

Visit
Tom's for a unique culinary
experience - Tom & staff will
assist in selection of the finest
beef, pork, indigenous NW seafoods, Tom's own
sausages and naturally smoked meats.

❊ ❊ ❊

Aldrich's Market is like no other .... it's a trip
back in time. Fun old toys, antiques, old phone
booth, and much more. You've got to see it. Add
old-fashioned service, regular & gourmet foods &
a fine wine selection.

Phones: Aldrich's 385-0500   Sally's 385-5794   Tom's 385-0501
Hours: Open every day from 7 a.m. till 10 p.m.

HOPPIN' JOHN

(Hoppin' John is traditionally served on New Year's Day down South)

2 cups blackeyed peas
4 strips of bacon or fatback
   (diced into small pieces)
1 cup rice

1 medium onion, chopped
1 hot red pepper
black pepper

Cook rice in salt water until done. Set aside.

Place the peas in a large pot, cover, cook with bacon, onion, red pepper and pepper. Cook until peas are tender, not mushy.

Add with the cooked rice, mix together.

Traditionally served with corn bread.

CHICKEN GUMBO   Usually served with corn bread.

2 pounds frying chicken
$\frac{1}{2}$ cup flour
$1\frac{1}{2}$ teaspoons salt
$\frac{1}{2}$ teaspoon pepper
$\frac{1}{2}$ cup shortening
2 cups okra
$\frac{1}{2}$ cup diced ham
$\frac{1}{2}$ cup chopped onions
$\frac{1}{2}$ cup chopped green peppers

$\frac{1}{2}$ cup chopped celery
1 clove garlic, crushed
2 cups canned tomatoes
$\frac{1}{2}$ cup water
1 teaspoon minced parsley
pinch thyme
$\frac{1}{2}$ bay leaf, crushed

Coat chicken pieces by shaking evenly 2 or 3 times in bag containing mixture of $\frac{1}{2}$ cup flour, $1\frac{1}{2}$ teaspoons salt, $\frac{1}{2}$ teaspoon pepper.

In soup pot, melt $\frac{1}{2}$ cup shortening, fry chicken pieces with skin side down first. Turn pieces when ready and cook till evenly brown. Remove chicken and set aside. Pour off and reserve fat.

Return 2 tablespoons of reserved fat to pot, add ham, garlic, onions, celery, green peppers and cook over medium heat until onions are transparent, stirring occasionally. Add okra, tomatoes, $\frac{1}{2}$ cup water, 1 teaspoon salt, 1 teaspoon cayenne pepper, $\frac{1}{2}$ teaspoon chili powder, thyme and bay leaf.

Return chicken to soup pot, simmer for about 25 minutes or until chicken is tender. Remove from heat, remove chicken pieces from gumbo. Return chicken to pot and cook 15 minutes longer.

If you're early for the Port Townsend ferry, park your car, camper or truck in the ferry area and walk on over to B. Joe's.... Burgers, dogs, Dreyer's ice cream, sandwiches, chicken, etc. The kids will love it, too. You'll be able to see the ferry coming in.

Dolly has recently started serving dinners, and since she's from the South, she usually includes some "down South" items.

She showed our staff the beginning of her own cook-book ideas combining memorabilia of the 20's 30's and 40's down south and some "mouthwatering" recipes.

BREAD AND ROSES TORTELLINI SOUP

¼ cup olive oil
½ head minced garlic
2 minced onions
3 stalks chopped celery
3 16 ounce cans tomatoes
2 cubes beef bouillon

2½ quarts water
¼ cup red wine
½ tablespoon fresh parsley or
    ¼ tablespoon dried parsley
2½ cups tortellini of your choice
parmesan cheese

Sauté in ¼ cup olive oil, the garlic, onion and celery, then add the 3 cans of tomatoes that have been crushed. Add water, wine and parsley.

Bring these all to a boil, then add 2½ cups tortellini and cook for 10 minutes before serving. Top with freshly ground parmesan cheese.

Makes 4 quarts.

CHOCOLATE MOUSSE PIE

6 ounces semi-sweet chocolate squares
¾ cup low fat milk
3 eggs
½ pint cream
2 tablespoons dry sherry
½ tablespoon cognac

Melt chocolate in ¼ cup low fat milk. Cool and add one at a time 3 egg yolks. Whip 2 egg whites stiff. Whip ½ pint cream stiff. Fold chocolate mixture into cream and then fold in egg whites. Mix in sherry and cognac. Chill. Whip ¼ pint of cream for top. Shave chocolate on top for garnish. Can be serve as individual mousse or placed in a baked pie shell.

Upon arriving at Bread and Roses Bakery, one's attention is captured by a meticulously groomed rose garden. The bakery is located in an old New England style building remarkable amidst the Victorian style architecture of this historic seaport town.

The bakery's assortment of quality fresh-baked breads, pastries and desserts combines with friendly service to provide a unique and pleasant experience. The daily soup and sandwich specials _are_ "special"!

Open Mon.- Sat. 7:30 a.m. till 6 p.m.
Sun. 7:30 a.m. till 4 p.m.

PASTA FOGOLORE

2 cups fresh mushrooms, sliced
½ cup onions, diced
1 cup ham, diced
2 cloves garlic, minced
¼ cup white wine
½ teaspoon oregano

1 pound fettuccine
5 eggs
½ teaspoon black pepper
⅓ cup parmesan cheese
2 tablespoons chopped parsley
1 tomato, diced
¼ cup olive oil

Sauté onion, mushrooms, ham and garlic in olive oil and white wine. In a large bowl combine oregano, eggs, pepper and parmesan cheese. Mix.

Place the fettuccine into boiling salted water to cover and cook to the desired degree of doneness. This should not require more than 8 or 9 minutes for al dente.

Then add sautéed vegetables and meat together with the pasta and mix well. Add tomatoes and parsley as garnishes. Serve hot.   Serves 4.

SALSA

1 number 6½ can diced tomatoes or
        14 medium tomatoes skinned and diced
2 large onions, diced
2 large green bell peppers, diced
6 jalapeno peppers (canned) and ¼ cup of juice
1 tablespoon salt
1 tablespoon cayenne pepper
2 tablespoons garlic powder
2 tablespoons ground cumin seeds
2 tablespoons fresh cilantro leaves

Dice jalapeno peppers, chop cilantro leaves, add to the onions and green peppers. Combine all ingredients and mix well. It is ready to serve.

Note: If freezing, let mixture sit overnight in refrigerator first.

Where the "locals" go..... you can watch the boats coming and going at Point Hudson (and the ferry).... right outside the window! You dine on fresh seafood, an assortment of sandwiches, special desserts, omelettes or are tempted by the "Daily Special". It's very informal, so bring the whole family. You will be pleased with the reasonable prices.

Open daily from 7 a.m. Breakfast and lunch every day.
Dinners Wednesday through Sunday, till 9 p.m.

HALIBUT SUPREME

6 ounces halibut filet
1 ounce bay shrimp
2 ounces sour cream

2 ounces cheddar cheese
1 egg
¼ cup half and half

Flour the filet, then dip in egg wash made of egg and half and half cream. Then pan fry halibut.

Top with sour cream, shrimp and cheddar cheese. Bake in a 350° oven for 10 minutes.

VEAL PARMESAN

4 ounces veal
4 ounces tomato sauce
1 egg
¼ cup half and half
2 ounces parmesan cheese

Flour the filet, then dip in egg wash made of egg and cream. Then pan fry veal.

Top with tomato sauce and parmesan.

Serve with a side of pasta.

Three levels of fine dining in one of Port Townsend's oldest historic downtown buildings.

Enjoy fresh seafood, steak and Italian specialties while relaxing in front of a grand waterfront window or in their cozy lounge.

Desserts are rich, and a special treat. Cocktails, beer and wine are served.

JOSH'S BREAD PUDDING

4 cups milk
1 cup sugar
1 cup milk
5 extra large eggs

pinch of salt
raisins
1 teaspoon pure vanilla
3 French rolls

Combine and heat 4 cups milk and 1 cup sugar to just below boiling. Then mix 1 cup milk, 5 eggs, salt and vanilla and pour into the hot liquid.

Butter 7 x 12 pan. Sprinkle raisins around bottom of pan, slice three French rolls into 3 pieces each and lay on top of raisins.

Pour liquid mixture over rolls and bake in a pan set inside another pan with ½ inch of water on bottom. Bake 23 minutes at 325° in convection oven. (30 minutes at 350° in conventional oven.)

Let cool 1 hour before serving.

RICE CUSTARD PUDDING

2½ cups milk
½ cup sugar
2 eggs
½ teaspoon vanilla

pinch of salt
½ cup raisins
1 cup cooked rice

Heat 2 cups milk and sugar together.
Whip ½ cup cold milk, 2 eggs, vanilla and salt. Add this to hot mixture. Then add raisins and cooked rice to liquid mixture, stir and pour into glass or stainless pan. Set in pan of water (1 inch deep) and bake for 45 minutes at 350°.

Josh Norris has been in the restaurant business in Port Townsend for about 25 years – and in this location for the past 3½ years.

He remarked that "you have to be crazy to be in this business for that long!", but he had a twinkle in his eye when he said it, and it was obvious that he was having fun.

The Little Red Kettle is snuggled between a candy shop and an antique shop inside one of Port Townsend's lovely old buildings.

Open seven days a week for breakfast, lunch and dinner.

CHEESY ARTICHOKE SOUP

2 tablespoons butter
2 tablespoons olive oil
2 carrots, diced
3 stalks celery, diced
2 onions, diced
1 green pepper, diced
1 teaspoon basil
1 teaspoon marjoram
1 teaspoon oregano
½ teaspoon rosemary
1 teaspoon dry mustard

½ cup flour
1 cup white wine
2 tablespoons white Worcestershire
1 teaspoon salt
1 teaspoon pepper
2 cups milk
3 cups diced artichoke hearts
2 cups grated sharp cheddar cheese
4 ounces cream cheese, diced
4 cups water (approx.) or stock
1 cup green onions, finely chopped

Sauté vegetables and herbs in butter and olive oil.

Mix flour, wine, Worcestershire, milk, salt, pepper in blender. Add slowly to vegetables. Cook on low until thick.

Add artichoke hearts and water. Heat. Add grated cheddar one handful at a time, stirring well.

Add diced cream cheese and stir until melted.

Serve topped with green onion. Serve with bread and butter.

SCALLOP POACH ORIENTAL

1½ ounces fresh shelled scallops
1 ounce mushrooms, sliced
1 ounce peas
½ ounce butter
pinch of garlic powder

pinch of ginger
dash of sherry
dash of white Worcestershire
2 large eggs, poached
1½ ounces Jack cheese, grated

Sauté mushrooms in butter and herbs until almost cooked.

Add scallops, peas, sherry and Worcestershire. Sauté until scallops are done. (Do not overcook.)

Place poached eggs in shallow bowl, blot off excess water. Spread cheese on both sides of bowl. Fill with sauté.

Serve with potatoes and toast.

Established in February 1982, the Salal Cafe is a co-operatively owned and managed enterprise. The risk, as well as the profit, is equally shared by all. The 20-plus members are a diverse group including artists, poets and publishers — all of whom love food and conversation.

Most foods are prepared fresh in the kitchen, using quality ingredients, or they are made locally. The Salal Cafe is located in the historic Franklin House building.

Open: breakfast Mon.- Fri. 7 till 11:30 a.m. Sat. 7 till noon. Sun. 7 till 2 p.m.
       lunch Mon.- Fri. 11:45 till 2 p.m.   Sat. 12:15 till 2:30 p.m.

POTATO SOUP

8 potatoes
4 tablespoons butter
2 chopped onions
2½ tablespoons flour
6 cups chicken broth

1 cup sour cream
1 cup half & half
¼ teaspoon white pepper
salt to taste

Peel potatoes, cut in quarters and simmer in water until tender, saving the potato water.

Melt butter in a pot, add onions and sauté until soft. Add flour to sautéed mixture until well blended. Add chicken broth, stirring until mixture thickens.

Mash potatoes until lumps are gone and stir into pot. Put soup in a blender until smooth. (If soup is too thick to blend, add a small amount of the potato water.)

Place back in pot and add the sour cream and half & half. If soup needs thinning, add some of the potato water. Heat to serving temperature.

Ladle into bowls and top with the condiments.

Condiments:

crispy bacon, crumbled
shredded cheddar cheese
green onion, thinly sliced

COCONUT PIE

1½ cups granulated sugar
2 eggs
½ teaspoon salt
1 cube margarine, softened
¼ cup flour (unsifted)

½ cup milk
1½ cups shredded coconut
1 tablespoon lemon juice
1 teaspoon vanilla extract

Beat eggs. Add sugar and salt, and beat until thick and lemon colored. Add flour and softened margarine beating in thoroughly. Slowly blend in milk. (Mixture will have a curdled appearance.)

Blend in lemon juice and vanilla extract. Stir in 1 cup shredded coconut. Pour into an unbaked pie shell. Sprinkle top with ½ cup coconut.

Bake at 350° for 45 to 60 minutes. Top with whipped cream.

P.S. The original recipe called for butter. However, I prefer margarine in this recipe.

The original Water Street Deli was down the street just a few blocks from its present location. The Needhams were able to expand to 4 times the space when they purchased the Kuhn Building.

The menu has also expanded and now includes a variety of soups, sandwiches and specialty desserts homemade by the owner, Sue Needham. It's soups are especially popular.

There is a wide assortment of beverages, beers and wines.

Open 7 days a week from 11 a.m. till 4 p.m.

It's only a 20 minute ferry ride from Mukilteo to Clinton (the southern end of Whidbey Island). This one island boasts of 5 state parks and recreation areas, 2 of which include historic forts and tourist centers. Highway 525 wends its way up through rural farms and miles of forest with views of water on both sides. So, after a look around Clinton, watch for the sign to Langley, a friendly town on a bluff with a scenic vista that goes on forever.

Traveling northward on 525, watch for Greenfield, with close-by vineyards on the historically recognized farm and now production site of the state's newest berry "Whidbey's Liqueur". There are tours and wine-tasting daily. Coupeville, overlooking the Saratoga Passage, has a great summer festival in its quaint downtown area.

Northward now to Fort Evey State Park, where the road turns east to Oak Harbor. Not only is there a bustling marina harbor that is half-way point for boaters from the Seattle-Tacoma area enroute to the San Juan Islands and Canada, but this is the home of Whidbey Naval Air Station.

You will never forget the breath-taking beauty from the Deception Pass bridge. Get out and walk over it...far below is the pounding surf of Puget Sound from one side of the bridge, while the view of islands, calm waterways and the mountains in the distance entranse one from the other side.

Leaving this, it is only a few turns before the road runs along a lake shore, with fishers and boaters almost always out. Anacortes is not far away now... gateway to the San Juan Islands by ferry.

Backtracking a few miles will get you on your way to LaConner...where thousands of photographs have been taken of the miles of daffodil and tulip fields each spring. LaConner boasts of many intriguing shops and a number of good restaurants.

It'll be a few miles to I-5 and a short hop to Everett, a great little city dating back to the 1890's when timber barons, railroad tycoons, lumberjacks and prospectors all helped shape its destiny. Situated on the protected shores of Puget Sound, the 2,000 slip harbor is the second biggest on the West Coast. Boeing assembly plant offers employment to many, and there is a tour available of the plant. If you would like an unusual tour, there is a trolley that can be chartered for a good trip around Everett- especially fun for the youngsters.

BW

SECTION 7

CLINTON: Madrona Restaurant
LANGLEY: Mike's Place, Peppers
OAK HARBOR: El Cazador, Kasteel Fransson
ANACORTES: Boomer's Landing, Captain's Place, Gere-a-deli
LA CONNER: Barkley's, The Black Swan, The Calico Cupboard
EVERETT: Klondike Kate's, Milwaukee Depot Cafe, Victor's
                Bacchus-by-the-Bay

CARROT PURÉE DIP

1½ pounds carrots
2 teaspoons paprika
2-4 cloves garlic, pressed
½ teaspoon ginger
1 tablespoon cumin, or to taste

salt and pepper
3 tablespoons wine vinegar
4 tablespoons olive oil
black olives

Peel carrots and boil in salted water until very soft. Drain and puree with spices, oil and vinegar. Make a day or 2 ahead of serving.

This is very beautiful and can be served with large croutons and fresh vegetables, especially green, red and yellow peppers. Garnish with black olives and parsley. A bonus to this recipe is that leftover dip with an equal amount of half and half or milk makes a most wonderful soup. We have added cashews and green pepper as garnish.

ROQUEFORT TART

6 ounces Roquefort cheese
3 ounces cream cheese
4 eggs

¾ cup half and half or
    whipping cream
grind of pepper and nutmeg

Prepare a crust in a flan or tart pan and sprinkle with lightly browned bread crumbs. Cream the cheeses and half & half together and beat in the eggs one at a time. Season with pepper and nutmeg. Pour into un-cooked crust and bake in the middle of the oven 45 to 50 minutes at 375° until tart is golden and firm. Remove rim and serve warm.

SEASONAL SALAD

To a basic salad of spinach, cabbage and other vegetables as available, add seasonal greens, flowers, herbs and weeds from field and garden. Here are some suggestions:

Herbs	Greens	Weeds	Flowers
chives	raddichio	sorrel	Johnny jump-ups
salad burnet	young beet greens	lamb's quarters	pansies
fennel	young kale	dandelion greens	calendula pedals
cilantro	arugula (rocket)	shepherd's purse	bachelor buttons
borage flowers	mustard	miner's lettuce	mustard flowers
mint	corn salad	vetch	nasturtiums
basil	orach		
parsley			

The Madrona — a warm, lively and unique restaurant — is located on scenic Whidbey Island in the historic Dodge Building near Clinton ferry terminal. Serving hearty soups, quiches, sandwiches, salads, baked goods and an assortment of beverages and coffees, the Madrona's sunny atmosphere appeals to both regulars and to tourists. A distinctive feature of the Madrona is its staff who run it as a cooperative, volunteer service endeavor in support of the Chinook Waldorf School. Adjacent to the Madrona is an outstanding, small bookstore, Warm Wind Books and Records. In summer the Madrona's hours are expanded — meals are catered for educational programs and special benefits.

Open Tues. thru Fri. 10:30 a.m. till 2:30 p.m.
Expanded hours during the summer.

EXTRA RICH BROWNIES

1 cup sifted flour	4 eggs, well beaten
½ teaspoon baking powder	4 squares semi-sweet chocolate
⅓ cup butter	1 teaspoon vanilla
2 cups sugar	½ cup walnuts, rough chopped

Melt chocolate with butter and remove from heat. Add sugar, then cool. Add well beaten eggs and vanilla. Mix well. Stir in flour, baking powder and walnuts.

Spread batter in greased and floured 9x13 inch pan. Bake in preheated 350° oven for 25 to 30 minutes.
While brownies are baking, prepare the following frosting:

Kahlua flavored frosting

1 square semisweet chocolate	1 teaspoon vanilla
2 tablespoons butter	2 tablespoons heavy cream
pinch of salt	powdered sugar
2 tablespoons Kahlua	

SPICED PEACH MOLD

6 ounces orange jello
1 teaspoon pumpkin pie spice
¼ cup vinegar
2 tablespoons sugar
1 13 oz. can sliced peaches
pinch salt
2 tablespoons cointreau
2 cups orange juice
1 cinnamon stick

Drain peaches and reserve. Boil vinegar, sugar, reserved juice, pumpkin spice and cinnamon stick for 10 minutes. Strain and add enough hot water to measure 2 cups. Add jello and dissolve. Add orange juice and chill until slightly firm, then add peaches and chill till firm.

You'll see Pepper's attractive sign first, because the restaurant is located inside a mini-mall called Ken's Corner..... about 2 miles north of the Clinton ferry.

Ann said "We serve fresh everything!" For example, there are home made pies, soups, salad dressings, muffins and a variety of desserts.

The atmosphere is pleasant and friendly - it's obvious that there are a lot of "regulars". A full bar and banquet room are available, with catering on and off premises to order.

Nightly enjoy a salad bar and choose from delectable specials... plus in-season fresh vegetables.

Open: 6:30 a.m. till 9:30 p.m. Tues. thru Sat.
8:00 a.m. till 8:00 p.m. Sun.   Closed Mon.

MIKE'S PLACE TURTLE CAKE   created by Iladeene Leierer

1 package (18½ ounces) chocolate cake mix that doesn't
    call for oil
20 ounces caramels
¼ cup butter
¾ cup evaporated milk
9 ounces real chocolate chips

chopped walnuts
flaked coconut
vanilla ice cream

Prepare cake mix according to package directions; pour half the batter into 9 x 13 inch baking pan and bake at 350° for 20 minutes.

Meanwhile, combine caramels and butter in saucepan and heat over low heat, stirring until mixture is melted and smooth; remove from heat and blend in milk. Pour evenly over baked cake layer and sprinkle evenly with chocolate chips. Cover with remaining cake batter. Sprinkle generously with walnuts, then add a generous sprinkling of coconut. Return pan to oven and bake another 20 minutes.

Serve warm with vanilla ice cream. Makes one 9x13 inch cake.

MIKE'S PLACE JAMBALAYA

Cajun seasoning mix*
2 cups rice
4 tablespoons butter
6 ounces sliced mesquite smoked
    sausage
1½ ounces salad shrimp

1½ cups diced ham
1½ cups chopped green onions
1½ cups chopped celery
1 cup chopped green bell peppers
4 cups chicken stock
1½ teaspoons garlic

Combine seasoning mix and set aside. Melt butter in a large frying pan over high heat, add ham and sausage and cook for 5 minutes. Add onions, celery, peppers, garlic and seasoning mix and stir well. Cook until browned. Stir in rice and cook for five minutes, add stock and cook over reduced heat until tender.

* Cajun seasoning mix

4 bay leaves
1 teaspoon salt
1 teaspoon white pepper
1 teaspoon dry mustard

1 teaspoon cayenne pepper
½ teaspoon ground cumin
½ teaspoon black pepper
½ teaspoon dried thyme leaves

Originally a feed and general store 70 years ago, Mike's Place today is a focal point in Langley.... with 59 seats and a staff of 35. Mike said "It's a melting pot" .... chefs from Seattle and further points wanting to get away from big cities... one lady who was with the old Olympic Hotel for years..... one chef formerly with a West German Officers Club doing Cajun.... a local woman with many years of restaurant experience creating Oriental and Chinese dishes.... and many more! It's a total team effort. After closing at night, prep people work thru the night, and a baker arrives early a.m. to begin her day. The staff opening the next morning find the baker still at work. Makes you want to see what it's all about, doesn't it?

Open 7 a.m. til 9 p.m. Sun. thru Thurs. Closes 10 p.m. Fri. & Sat.

SALSA DE BURRITOS

2 green bell peppers
4 tomatoes
2 carrots
1½ yellow or white onions
1 bunch cilantro

salt to your taste
black pepper to your taste
3 cloves garlic, chopped fine
1 can tomato juice

Dice all the vegetables, then fry them with vegetable oil, along with the spices. When they are turning a little brown, add tomato juice and some chicken base, and just a touch of sugar (about 3 tablespoons) and let it boil for about 1 hour. Have fun using this for all kinds of burritos.

SALSA DE AROS POLLO

3 tomatoes
½ yellow or white onion
3 dried mild peppers
2 cloves garlic, finely chopped
1½ cups flour
orange juice

white pepper to taste
salt to taste
very little chili powder
very little paprika (just for color)
tomato juice

Boil the tomatoes with the onions and the dried peppers. Then blend them to make a paste with the garlic and the spices.

Fry your flour in about 1½ tablespoons of oil. When it is brown, mix your paste with the spices, then add some tomato juice and a little bit of orange juice. Let it boil for ½ hour. It is ready.

El Cazador Restaurant is family-owned and operated, and Aurelio Rodriguez said that they take special pride in the freshness of all food.

The first El Cazador Mexican Restaurant was opened in 1982... now there are three — Anacortes, Burlington and Oak Harbor. Soon there will be the fourth — in Sequim.

So relax in their Mexican setting, take advantage of the special friendly service and enjoy one of their memorable meals!

Open: 11 a.m. till 10 p.m. Mon.-Thurs.   Fri. & Sat. till 11 p.m.
Open: noon till 10 p.m. Sunday.

FILET OF SOLE AMSTERDAM
Created by Jean Paul for Kasteel Franssen Restaurant

8 filets of Petrali or Dover sole
12 mussels
½ pound mushrooms
1 cup dry vermouth

2 egg yolks
lemon juice
butter
flour, tarragon, salt, pepper
whipping cream

Preheat oven to 375°.

In buttered ovenware dish put 8 filets of sole, pour over them 1 cup of dry vermouth and 2 tablespoons lemon juice. Salt and pepper to taste. Cover with foil and put in oven 5 to 7 minutes, until fish flakes easily with fork.

In skillet sauté 1 cup of sliced mushrooms in butter and sprinkle with a pinch of tarragon, then add 12 poached mussels.

When fish is done, drain liquid into a sauce pan and reduce. Mix 1 tablespoon butter with 1 tablespoon flour, add reduced fish liquid. Blend. Pour over fish. Beat one egg yolk mixed with two tablespoons of cream. Pour over fish, then glaze under broiler. Serve with rice pilaf.

TRIFLE

4 slices angelfood or pound cake
4 tablespoons raspberry jam
¼ cup sherry

¼ cup brandy
½ teaspoon vanilla

1. In a deep dish, put 4 slices of cake, pour sherry and brandy over cake and let soak for 10 minutes. Spread with 4 tablespoons of raspberry jam.
2. Make thick pastry cream.* When it is cool, pour it over the cake. Whip cream and make border around the dish. Sprinkle with slivered toasted almonds.

* Thick pastry cream

1 cup milk
3 egg yolks

½ teaspoon vanilla
⅓ cup sugar

Scald 1 cup of milk in stainless steel sauce pan; combine and add 3 egg yolks, ⅓ cup sugar, ½ teaspoon vanilla.

Beat until thick and pale, put in double boiler. Gradually add the hot milk and cook, stirring rapidly for a few minutes until cream is smooth and thick. Cool off by rolling the cream for 10 minutes with spoon.   4 servings

This charming restaurant, at the Auld Holland Inn is designed after castles in the south of Holland. The doors opened in 1984, and since that time the Kasteel has provided Whidbey Island with the finest of European and American cuisine. The dishes are prepared under the watchful eye of Jean Paul Combettes who was born in France and has 60 years of culinary experience. He is truly a legend in his own time!

The old Dutch theme is carried throughout the restaurant with antiques and old-world museum prints.

The Kasteel Franssen also features a banquet room that will accomodate up to 150 guests; and a cozy lounge and piano bar. Restaurant hosts are the Franssens... Joe, Elisa, Peter, Carl & Michael.

Open 5:30 till 9:30 p.m. for dining.

STEAMED PINK SCALLOPS

1 pound fresh in the shell pink scallops
2 ounces butter
2 ounces dry vermouth
1 sprig fresh parsley
1 green onion, chopped
1 clove garlic, minced
pinch of pepper

Place all ingredients in a pan with a tight fitting lid. Steam until just done (about 2 – 3 minutes) or until the center of the scallops start to turn opaque.

Pour scallops and all of the liquid into a serving bowl. Serve with drawn butter and a loaf of sourdough bread.

HOT SEAFOOD SALAD

6 ounces favorite seafoods (such as
    bay scallops, shrimp, crab)
½ slice bacon
2 ounces sliced mushrooms
2 ounces sliced zucchini
1 ounce Julienned sweet red
    or yellow peppers
½ ounce diced yellow onion
1 clove garlic, minced
2 ounces dry vermouth

2 ounces whole butter
½ ounce parmesan cheese, grated
½ tomato cut into wedges
2 ounces chopped green onion
1 squeeze fresh lemon
pinch of thyme
salt and pepper to taste
fresh torn greens

Have available and ready to serve – 2 cups of fresh, torn and chilled greens.

Sauté bacon until it just begins to brown. Add scallops or any other raw seafood and cook about half done. Add mushrooms, sweet peppers, diced yellow onion and continue cooking until onion turns translucent. Add zucchini, minced garlic, squeeze of lemon and thyme.

When pan returns to hot and begins to simmer, add shrimp and crab.

Flame with vermouth and add whole butter. Cook until seafood is done, and sauce begins to slightly thicken. Season if desired. Ladle over greens. Sprinkle with parmesan cheese and green onion. Garnish with tomato wedges. Makes one entrée sized salad or 4 first course servings.

Boomers' Landing is a waterfront restaurant overlooking Guemes Channel, where you may enjoy a passing parade of yachts; see in-bound tankers navigate the channels to local oil refineries; watch freighters load logs bound for the Orient or simply bask in the waning glow of a sunset over the San Juan Islands.
Chef/owner Hank Thompson specializes in creative seafoods purchased fresh from local boats.

Hank features pink scallops, spot prawns, mussels, salmon and Dungeness crab.

CALAMARI

1 pound squid (cleaned)
2 cups all purpose flour
1 teaspoon salt

$\frac{1}{4}$ teaspoon pepper
1 teaspoon paprika

AIOLI SAUCE

1 cup mayonnaise
$\frac{1}{3}$ cup garlic (fresh, chopped)
$\frac{1}{2}$ teaspoon lemon juice

$\frac{1}{2}$ teaspoon tarragon
$\frac{1}{2}$ teaspoon Dijon mustard

Preparation

1. Mix mayonnaise, chopped garlic, lemon juice, tarragon and Dijon mustard. Blend well and refrigerate.
2. Sift flour, salt, pepper and paprika into shallow bowl. Set aside.
3. Rinse cleaned squid in cold water and separate body from tentacles by slicing in half just above beak area.
4. Cut squid's body section lengthwise (leaving connected at tip) about $\frac{1}{8}$ inch cuts.
5. Toss body and legs in seasoned flour. Coat well.
6. Cook floured squid in hot oil (350°) about 30 seconds. <u>Do not overcook</u>!!!
7. Serve with Aioli sauce and fresh lemon juice.

MEDALLIONS OF PORK TENDERLOIN

2 pounds pork tenderloin
$\frac{1}{4}$ cup oil
3 teaspoons chopped shallots
4 ounces Madeira
$1\frac{2}{3}$ cups Demiglaze (rich brown sauce)
3 cups sliced mushrooms

1. Cut pork into 1 ounce chunks, place each chunk between wax paper and pound until they are about $\frac{1}{4}$ inch thick medallions.
2. Heat oil in pan until it will ripple on the sides.
3. Brown each medallion on both sides, put on a serving plate.
4. Sauté shallots and mushrooms lightly, add Madeira and let this reduce to about half the volume, stir in Demiglaze until sauce is bubbling and thick.
5. Pour hot sauce over pork medallions and serve.

The Captain's Place Restaurant is one of the best kept secrets in Anacortes, but it's worth the effort to find it.

There's waterfront dining, delicious homemade food using the freshest fish, meats and produce. The staff is friendly, and the atmosphere is warm and comfortable. In the summer there is dining on the patio.

Their staff is trained to prepare meals for restricted diets: diabetic, low cholesterol, vegetarian, etc. They do not add sulfites, msg or other preservatives.

They want each guest to know that he or she is the most important part of the restaurant.

Open: Tues.- Sat. 11 a.m. till 9 p.m.   Sun. brunch 10 - 3 p.m. summers
Sunday dinner 5 - 8 p.m.   Closed Monday.

GRANDMA SUE'S HOT FUDGE SUNDAE SAUCE

3 ounces unsweetened chocolate
¼ cup butter
1½ cups powdered sugar

9 tablespoons evaporated milk
dash of salt
½ teaspoon vanilla

Melt chocolate and butter in double boiler. Blend in sugar, milk, salt and vanilla. Simmer for ½ hour. Serve over your favorite ice cream sundae, banana split or Mudd Pie.

SOUVLAKA ARNI   (Greek Pita Sandwich)

3 pounds roast beef, cubed
    or sliced
⅓ cup lemon juice
3 tablespoons olive oil
1 teaspoon salt
1 tablespoon oregano

2 cloves garlic, pressed
¼ teaspoon pepper
2 green peppers, chopped
1 onion, grated

Mix together and marinate overnight. Cook until beef is done. Serve warm stuffed inside Greek pita bread. Add lettuce, tomato, Greek olives and sour cream.   Use the following peperoncini sauce.

PEPERONCINI SAUCE

2 cups ripe tomatoes, diced
2 onions (white or red) diced

2 cups Greek peppers (peperoncini)
1 cup favorite Italian dressing

Dice the peppers. Mix together. Serve over Greek pita sandwich.

Gere-a-Deli & Bistro is located in historic downtown Anacortes in the Old Bank Building. Established in 1981 by Laurie and Phil Gere, the Bistro has a delightful European ambiance and is filled with antiques and colorful prints. It is noted for good homey food and drink that helps make this a friendly neighborhood gathering place.

Hearty soups, homemade desserts, great deli sandwiches, pasta dishes, garden fresh salads, espresso, micro-brewery ales and Washington wines are all featured here.

Summer: Open daily 9 a.m. till 9 p.m.
Winter: Open Monday through Saturday 9 a.m. till 4 p.m.

BARKLEY'S WHITE CHOCOLATE MOUSSE

6 ounces white chocolate
3 tablespoons whipping cream
1 teaspoon vanilla
$\frac{1}{4}$ cup brandy

$\frac{1}{8}$ cup sugar
3 egg whites, room temp.
1$\frac{1}{2}$ cups whipping cream
whipped cream for garnish

1. In a double boiler, melt chocolate over hot, not boiling, water. Remove from heat and stir in 3 tablespoons cream and vanilla. Set aside.
2. In a small saucepan, heat brandy and sugar to boiling. Remove from heat and stir into chocolate mixture.
3. In a large mixing bowl, beat egg whites until stiff but not dry. Gently fold chocolate mixture into egg whites.
4. Whip the 1$\frac{1}{2}$ cups cream until stiff and fold into chocolate mixture. Pour into individual parfait glasses. Cover and chill at least 4 hours. Garnish with whipped cream.   6 to 8 servings

SESAME RED CABBAGE AND PEAPODS

Garlic Butter (see below)
2 pounds red cabbage, cut into 2" squares.
$\frac{1}{2}$ cup chicken stock
6 ounces fresh or frozen Chinese pea pods, snapped and strung
2 tablespoons sesame oil
salt and pepper to taste

1. Prepare Garlic Butter and set aside.
2. In a large skillet, over high heat, cook cabbage in chicken stock. Add salt and pepper and cook until cabbage is tender-crisp.
3. Add peapods to cabbage. Cover pan for 3-4 minutes or until peapods are slightly cooked or (in the case of the frozen produce) just warmed through. Add Garlic Butter and sesame oil to cabbage mixture and toss gently. Serve immediately.   6 to 8 servings

Garlic Butter

1 cube (4 oz.) butter at room temperature
5 cloves garlic, minced
1 teaspoon Worcestershire sauce
1 tablespoon cognac
2 tablespoons fresh chopped parsley

Barkley's specializes in Northwest Cuisine, drawing from the produce of the Skagit Valley and the bounty of Puget Sound. Chef-proprietor Michael Hood is a world-traveled native who is somewhat of a local character and adds color to his very charming dining room.

Barkley's is well-reviewed regionally and nationally, reservations are a must – especially on weekends. It is moderately priced, and there is a full bar.

Open: Lunch Mon.-Sat. 11:30 till 3 p.m.
          Dinner nightly at 5 p.m.   Sunday brunch 10 till 3 p.m.

KASLER NORTHWOODS BLACK SWAN

Kasler, a German-style smoked pork loin, can be obtained at most German meat markets. Pork chops can be used with equally satisfying results.

1 rib per person (Kasler)
2 tablespoons oil
Walla Walla sweet onions (or
     Bermuda onions)
Golden Delicious apples
1 tablespoon pine nuts

fresh (or dried) morel mushrooms
1 bottle Mount Baker Muller Thurgau
     (or German Riesling) wine
currant preserves
sour cream

1. Preheat oven to 350°.
2. Cut Kasler into individual ribs, flour, shake off excess flour. Brown in hot oil, then remove to baking pan.
3. To hot oil add minced Walla Walla sweet onions (½ cup per rib). Sauté until opaque. Add sliced Golden Delicious apples (one apple per rib) and 1 tablespoon pine nuts (one tablespoon per rib). Sauté lightly.
4. To pan add 3 or 4 fresh whole morels (or dried or canned morels). Wilt lightly, then pour mixture over Kasler in baking pan. Pour Muller Thurgau over (to cover) the Kasler. Cover the dish with foil and bake for 30 minutes.
5. When done, remove Kasler to serving platter. Place a strainer over a large sauce pan and pour the rest of mushroom/apple mixture into the strainer. The strainer will catch the mixture. Pour the mixture over the Kasler on the serving platter. Keep warm.
6. To the cooking juices in the sauce pan, add 2 tablespoons currant preserves and 1 cup sour cream. Heat and blend. Simmer 10 minutes. Pour sauce over the Kasler.

FRESH HALIBUT WITH RHUBARB SAUCE

2 8-ounce halibut filets
1 cup fish stock or water
1 Walla Walla sweet onion, chopped
½ cup white wine
1 tablespoon butter

1 tablespoon butter
1 teaspoon garlic, crushed
2 stalks fresh rhubarb, chopped
1 tablespoon strawberry vinegar
4 tablespoons creme fraîche or sour
     cream

Poach halibut filets in fish stock or water with onion, wine, butter and garlic. Remove fish from stock and keep warm. Add rhubarb and vinegar to the stock. Simmer until rhubarb is completely tender, about 5 minutes.

Force sauce through a food mill or strainer. Add creme fraîche or sour cream and blend well.

Cover bottom of serving dish with sauce and place halibut on top. Serve with extra sauce on the side.

The Black Swan, in the channelside town of La Conner, is snuggled into a cozy building on the busy "downtown" area... the dining area recently expanded. It is noted for innovative combinations as well as use of traditional European styles — with seasonal menus featuring fresh local ingredients. Seafood is emphasized, either simply prepared with fresh herbs or orchestrated into a bouillabaisse, paella or a pirate's stew. Seasonally, the choice may be a salad of edible flowers and foraged greens, wild sorrel to sauce oysters or possibly crisp spring nettles to compliment fresh local lamb. Decadent desserts, homemade gelato, espresso and fine wines are also available.
No smoking.

Hours are seasonal.

CURRIED SPLIT PEA SOUP

1 cup cooked brown rice
½ cup butter
1 large onion
1 large clove garlic
1 pound green split peas
3 cups water
3 cups chicken broth
2 teaspoons curry powder

1 teaspoon salt
½ teaspoon oregano
2 teaspoons tamari
   (or soy sauce)
½ teaspoon ground white pepper
1¼ cups half & half
   (or milk)

1. Sauté onion and garlic in butter till soft.
2. Add water, chicken broth and split peas. Bring to boil, reduce heat.
3. Add seasonings, cover, then simmer approximately 1 hour or until peas are tender.
4. Remove from heat and stir in cooked rice.
5. Purée mixture in a blender or food processor.
6. Return mixture to saucepan. Add half and half. Heat just till serving temperature. Do not boil.
7. Serve.

MULLIGATAWNY SOUP

Chicken broth (reserve cooked chicken)
¼ cup butter
1 large onion, chopped
1 large carrot, diced
1 cup celery, diced
1 green pepper, chopped
3 tablespoons flour

1 teaspoon curry powder
½ teaspoon nutmeg
dash cayenne pepper
¼ teaspoon chili powder
2 tablespoons chopped fresh
   parsley
² cup raw white rice
2 apples, peel, slice thin

1. Strain chicken broth, cool, reserve chicken. Return broth to large pot and bring to a boil
2. Sauté vegetables in butter till tender. Add flour and herbs. Stir till vegetables are well coated.
3. Add vegetables to the broth, along with tomatoes and rice. Bring to a boil, cover and reduce heat. Simmer till rice is tender.
4. Add apple slices and diced chicken.

The Calico Cupboard, located at the foot of South First Street, abounds with old country flavor... antiques, old prints, memorabilia and waitresses in ruffled pinafores.

There is quite often a little wait (especially on weekends), but it's worth the wait! Their bakery items are inspired ..... nutty cinnamon rolls, pecan tarts, carrot muffins, shortcake-raspberry bars, currant scones, date bearclaws.... just to name a few of the delectables that await you!

Open every day from 8 a.m. till 5 p.m.
Open weekdays in the summer from 7 a.m.

BACCHUS BY THE BAY HOUSE DRESSING

1 cup Spanish olive oil
¼ cup cider vinegar
¼ cup sugar

2 tablespoons Worcestershire
2 tablespoons onion, finely chopped
1 egg

In small mixing bowl, combine olive oil, vinegar, sugar, Worcestershire, onion and egg. Blend together until smooth. Use as is over salad greens garnished with bacon bits, water chestnuts and sprouts; or heat for use on wilted spinach salads and garnish with shrimp and toasted almonds. Makes about 1¾ cups dressing.

PATÉ ALFREDO

1 pound chicken livers
1 cup milk
¼ cup brandy
2½ sticks butter (1¼ cups)
    at room temperature
1 yellow onion, sliced

1 Granny Smith apple, peeled
    and cored
¼ cup sherry
¼ cup heavy cream
1¼ teaspoons salt
1 teaspoon fresh lemon juice

Melt one cube butter in large skillet. Add onion and apple, sauté until very soft and golden. Transfer to food processor with a slotted spoon. Drain livers, discard milk they have been soaking in and add to skillet. Sauté about 10 minutes or until livers are no longer pink. Add to onion mixture in processor. Add sherry to skillet and deglaze.

Add pan juices, salt and cream to processor and puree until very smooth. Cool slightly before adding the rest of the butter (1½ cubes) and lemon juice and process thoroughly

Pour into one large or several small ramekins. Refrigerate. An aspic glaze may be put on top the next day to give it a finished look. Heat 1½ cups white wine or apple juice with one envelope Knox gelatin. Cool over ice water once gelatin has dissolved. Decorate paté with bits of bright tomato skin and green onion pieces and top with the aspic. Refrigerate until set.

Serve with crackers or toasted french bread, and apple slices.

Al Frederickson's <u>Bacchus by the Bay</u> is a bustling, friendly omelette house each morning and has candlelight dining in the evening. Each summer the Bayside patio opens for lunching on the beautiful shores of Port Gardner Bay. The olde-world style pub features Washington's micro-brews on tap and an extensive wine list. There's a fashion show every Wednesday noon and live music in the pub Friday and Saturday nights.

Open every day from 6 a.m. till midnight.

CAJUN COD

8 ounce piece of cod
2 ounces sliced onions
2 ounces sliced green peppers
2 ounces oil

2 ounces white wine
1 teaspoon flour
cajun spice (see recipe)

Dip cod in cajun spice to cover both sides completely. Place in frying pan, add oil, wine, onion and peppers. Sprinkle flour over cod.

Bake for 12 to 15 minutes. Remove cod from pan.

Cook sauce for 2 minutes over medium heat. Pour sauce over cod...enjoy.

CAJUN SPICE

1 cup sugar
$\frac{1}{4}$ cup cayenne pepper
5 tablespoons granulated garlic
$\frac{1}{2}$ cup paprika

$\frac{1}{2}$ cup salt
$\frac{1}{4}$ cup chili powder
3 tablespoons rosemary
3 tablespoons thyme

KATE'S HONEY DILL DRESSING

$\frac{1}{2}$ cup mayonnaise
$\frac{1}{4}$ cup sour cream
$1\frac{1}{2}$ cups buttermilk (to thin)
3 teaspoons tarragon

dill (to taste)
2 tablespoons lemon juice
1 teaspoon granulated garlic
2 tablespoons honey (or to taste)

Blend thoroughly and let stand for several hours in refrigerator to allow flavors to blend.

Klondike Kate's Restaurant and Lounge is in the historic McCabe building, which is conveniently located next to Interstate 5. When you visit Kate's, you will experience turn of the century atmosphere, combined with excellent food and drinks. An abundant menu – prime rib, steaks, seafood, poultry, spare ribs – all prepared by their Master Chef. You can enjoy a libation of your choice or fine wine – moderately priced.

There is dancing on Friday and Saturday nights.

Mon.-Fri. Breakfast 6 a.m. till 11 a.m.   Lunch 11 a.m. till 3 p.m.
Early diner dinner 3 p.m. till 5 p.m.
Mon.-Thurs. Dinner 5-10 p.m.   Fri.-Sat. 5-11 p.m. Sun. 4-9 p.m.

BOB'S SPECIAL CHILI

1 pound ground beef
1 medium onion
2 stalks celery
2 or 3 cloves garlic
4 cups cooked red beans
1 teaspoon allspice

1 teaspoon paprika
3 tablespoons chili powder
2 teaspoons salt
10 ounces tomato sauce
10 ounces cooked tomatoes

Brown beef, then add diced onion, diced celery and garlic and cook until limp. Put all ingredients in a casserole, stir well.

Bake in 300° oven for one hour.
Top with grated cheddar cheese and serve.

BLUEBERRY PANCAKES

2 cups of biscuit mix
1 egg
1 cup milk
1 cup water
1 packet of dry yeast

Mix all ingredients well and let stand for 30 minutes.

Cook on oiled griddle. Sprinkle blueberries on top before turning.
What could be easier?

Steeped in nostalgia, this restaurant is located in the original train depot—built in 1912 and owned by the Milwaukee Railroad Company until it went out of business in 1980. Old train photographs and local old pictures adorn the walls.

Bob Carley has owned the establishment since 1985...and plans to expand in the near future into the old train baggage area.

Bob buys local farm products and serves local berry jam.

Open: Mon. 6 a.m. till 3 p.m.   Tues. thru Sat. 6 a.m. till 9 p.m.
      Sun. 8 a.m. till 2 p.m.

SEAFOOD SALAD SAUTÉ

2½ ounces chopped bacon
4 large prawns, peeled
     and deveined
8 large scallops
6 ounces bay shrimp
½ cup Chablis
2 or 3 ounces green pepper
2 or 3 ounces red pepper
2 ounces yellow onion

3 ounces zucchini
3 ounces yellow squash
4 tomato quarters
4 ounces bacon dressing
1 head romaine
1¼ ounces 1000 Island dressing
1 ounce shredded parmesan
2 lemon wedges

In bowl – toss romaine pieces and 1000 Island dressing and place half
of the romaine on each plate.
Sauté bacon until crisp. Add prawns, scallops and shrimp.
Sauté approximately 2 minutes.
Julienne the green and red peppers, yellow onion, zucchini and yellow
squash. Add these vegetables and cook for 1 minute.
Add white wine and bacon dressing, then stir or toss while cooking.
Add tomato wedges.
Spread your seafood sauté over salad and sprinkle shredded parmesan.
Serve with lemon wedges.   Serves 2.

VICTOR'S BURNT CREAM

6 egg yolks
2 cups granulated sugar
5 tablespoons pure vanilla extract
1 pint + 2 fluid ounces pasteurized whipping cream

Preheat oven to 325 degrees. Mix together in medium bowl egg yolks,
sugar, vanilla extract and whipping cream. Place six custard cups into
a roasting pan. Fill custard cups ¾ full of custard mixture.

Pour 1 to 1½ gallons warm water into roasting pan to surround the 6
custard cups. Place in oven. Bake 45 minutes.

Topping for custard

1 cup granulated sugar
2 teaspoons ground cinnamon

Remove custard from oven and sprinkle 1 teaspoon of sugar/cinnamon
mixture over top of each custard cream, return to oven and bake
another 20 minutes.

Remove cups from roasting pan and let cool for 2 hours in refrigerator.

Serve with whipped cream (optional).   Serves 6

Victor's — elegant surroundings
and delicious cuisine at affordable prices... a menu
that suits every taste, from a chef's "more-than-a-Burger" to a special preparation
of Roast Duckling. Whether it's a casual meal or celebrating a special occasion,
Victor's has a reputation for friendly service and satisfied customers.

My cooking experience started abruptly at age thirteen when my mother accepted a full-time job and left the dinner planning and cooking for our family of five to me.

MAYONNAISE CAKE

¾ cup mayonnaise
1 cup sugar
3 tablespoons ground chocolate
1 teaspoon cinnamon
1 teaspoon vanilla
½ teaspoon salt
2 cups flour
1 cup raisins
1 cup nuts
1 cup boiling water
1 teaspoon baking soda

This recipe was from the World War 2 time.... about <u>everything</u> was rationed. Sometimes we could get mayonnaise when there were shortages of oil or eggs. It's still a favorite.

1. Dissolve soda in boiling water, then pour water over raisins and nuts and let stand 5 to 10 minutes.
2. Sift sugar, cinnamon and chocolate and mix with mayonnaise.
3. Add water, nuts and riasins and blend well.
4. Sift flour and salt together and add to mayonnaise mixture.
5. Add vanilla, blend well.
6. Bake in preheated 350° oven in greased, floured tin for approx. 50 minutes.

Grandma never wasted <u>anything</u>! This was an answer to using old bread and sour milk.... and they're good.

GRANDMA'S OVERNIGHT HOT CAKES

2 cups stale bread
2 cups sour milk*

Soak bread in milk overnight.   * To sour the milk, add a little vinegar to milk and let set 10 minutes.

In the morning, beat thoroughly the above mixture. Add 4 beaten egg yolks. Then add:

1 teaspoon baking soda
½ teaspoon salt

2 tablespoons sugar
1 tablespoon butter

To all of the above, add 1 cup flour and 1 stiffly beaten egg white. Cook hotcakes.

Tastes like both pancakes and French toast. (I use whole wheat flour.)

Almost 10 years ago I received a phone call to do calligraphy for one of my clients who was planning a buffet dinner for over 200. I ended up doing the invitation and catering the whole dinner (with the help of my brother and sister-in-law.) The event was a great success — we had 5 or 6 people ask for our catering card! This was one of the desserts that day.

WHISKEY BALLS

pinch of salt
3 cups vanilla wafer crumbs
2 heaping tablespoons cocoa
½ cup powdered sugar

¼ cup white corn syrup
1 cup chopped nuts
½ cup whiskey

Combine ingredients and shape into balls. Roll in powdered sugar.

Another catering job was for a wedding reception for 125. This is the recipe for one tray of open-faced finger sandwiches that day.

Some were on crackers and some were on assorted breads. Garnishes were slice of olive, thinly sliced bell pepper or cucumber, nasturium petals or touch of parsley.

HORS D'OEUVRES SANDWICH SPREAD

½ green bell pepper
1 clove garlic
½ pound Tillamook cheese

1 small jar chipped beef
1 small can hot sauce
1 egg

Put bell pepper, chipped beef, cheese, and garlic through grinder. Add can of hot sauce, 1 beaten egg and cook for ½ hour in double boiler. Keep in refrigerator until ready to use.

Makes 1 pint

No story to this — just one of my son, Gene's favorites.

SWEET AND SOUR HAMBURGERS

1 pound ground beef
1½ pounds pork sausage
1 teaspoon salt
¼ teaspoon pepper
1 large onion, sliced

2 tablespoons soy sauce
½ cup water
¼ cup vinegar
½ cup brown sugar

1. Mix beef, pork sausage, salt and pepper together and form into 6 large patties.
2. Brown both sides in ungreased frying pan.
3. Add sliced onions.
4. Mix soy, water, vinegar and brown sugar and pour over.
5. Cover and simmer until hamburger and onions are done (about 15 minutes).

Serves 6.

MUSHROOM SOUP

1 pound chopped mushrooms
1 small minced onion
2 tablespoons tomato paste
a little minced garlic

2 ounces sweet vermouth
3 cups chicken broth
3 egg yolks
2 tablespoons parmesan cheese

Sauté mushrooms and onions. Add tomato paste and garlic and cook a little longer. Add sweet vermouth and chicken broth. Heat.

Add beaten egg yolks and cheese to a small amount of the heated broth and return to the soup. Top with parsley and serve.

COLE SLAW

$\frac{1}{4}$ cup cider vinegar
$\frac{1}{4}$ cup sugar
1 teaspoon celery seeds
1 teaspoon dill weed
1 medium size head cabbage

1 green pepper, chopped fine
1 small onion, chopped fine
1 cup apples, chopped
$\frac{1}{4}$ cup sunflower seeds
$\frac{1}{2}$ cup mayonnaise

Shred cabbage. In a pan combine vinegar, sugar, celery seeds and bring to a boil, stirring until sugar is dissolved. Cool.

Combine all ingredients and refrigerate at least 2 hours before serving.

TABBOULI SALAD

1 cup bulgur, uncooked
2 cups boiling water
½ cup olive or vegetable oil
¼ cup lemon juice
½ teaspoon salt
½ teaspoon pepper
1 cup parsley, chopped fine
½ cup green onions and tops,
   chopped
2 tomatoes, diced

3 teaspoons vinegar, optional
¼ to ½ cup chopped olives,
   green or black
½ cup celery, diced
½ cup cheese, diced
1 medium cucumber, diced
3 hardboiled eggs, chopped
½ cup sunflower seeds
1 to 1½ cups leftover meats*
½ to 1 cup leftover vegetables*

Poul boiling water over bulgur in large bowl. Let stand 1 hour.
Drain well in colander and return to bowl. Add remaining ingredients and mix well. Chill at least 2 hours. Serve on lettuce.

*Left over meats: roast beef, chicken, tongue, ham, sausage
*Vegetables: raw or cooked. Peas, carrots, broccoli, cauliflower
(or you may come up with other additions.)

*You'll probably think of lots of other left-overs; I often
add more on the second or third day.*

Index

Clark's Glazed Chicken	40	Kalbi Salmon	98
Oriental Chicken Salad	62	Salmon Bisque	42
Paté Alfredo	174	Salmon Bisque	30
Stuffed Poulet	72	Tasty Sauté of Sole	40
		Vera Cruz Style Red Snapper	28

BEEF

Barbecue Ribs	128
Beef Stroganoff	82
New York Whiskey Steak	52
Pepper Pan Roast	70
Roast Prime Rib of Beef	86
Steak Kiev	46
Sweet & Sour Hamburgers	184
Tournedos Royal	22
Veal Parmesan	142

PORK

Chinese Barbecued Pork	46
Kasler Northwoods	170
Medallions of Pork Tenderloin	164

FISH

Baked Red Snapper Florentine	36
Baked Salmon	44
Blackened Salmon	118
Cajun Cod	176
Chilled Halibut Steak	50
Filet of Sole Amsterdam	160
Florentine Salmon	48
Fresh Halibut with Rhubarb Sauce	170
Gardner's Salmon	66
Halibut Dijonnaise	90
Halibut Rainier	80
Halibut Supreme	142
Halibut Rainier	80
Joe's Fritata	124

SEAFOOD

Avocado Melt	90
Baked Oysters Pleasant Beach	116
Bushwhacker Cajun Shrimp	20
Bushwhacker Oysters Rockefeller	20
Calamari	164
Clam Chowder	100
Clam Patties	126
Crab & Cheese Stuffed Prawns	98
Crab Leg Ambassador	110
Crab & Shrimp Sauté	128
Crab Stilton	36
Geoduc	34
Gorgeous Prawn Sauté	74
Halibut in Parchment	124
Hap's Clam Chowder	58
Hot Seafood Salad	162
Joe's Fritata	124
Michael Murphy's Oysters al Pesto	68
Northwest Sauté	70
Oysters Matriciana	68
Oysters Poulsbo Creek	114
Pickled Shrimp in Beer	30
Sauteéd Barbecued Prawns	44
Scallop Poach Oriental	146
Scampi	130
Seafood Fettuccine	64
Seafood Salad Sauté	180
Seafood Sauté	50
Smoked Salmon Salad	72
Steamed Pink Scallops	162

CHILI

Boatshed Chili	104
Bob's Special Chili	178
Chili Beans	32

CHEESE

Amaretto Cheese cake	84
Lemon-Honey Cheese cake	78
Lighthouse Cheese cake	102
Fettuccine Salsiccia	26
Nachos	28
Roquefort Tart	152

BREADS

Apple Muffin	62
Blueberry Pancakes	178
Gingerbread	78
Grandma's Overnight Pancakes	183
Honey Bread	108
Old-fashioned Biscuits	82
Sunday Brunch Scones	74
Toasted Seasoned Bagels	102

BREAKFAST ITEMS

Blueberry Pancakes	178
Eggs Nicole	16
Grandma's Overnight Pancakes	183
Koryuffin	16
Wheat-free Granola	120

CAKES

Carrot Cake	88
Coffee Cake	24
Mayonnaise Cake	182
Mike's Place Turtle Cake	156

DESSERTS

Almond Tarte	22
Barkley's White Chocolate Mousse	168
Blueberry Buckle	106
Chocolate, Chocolate Chip Cheese cake	96
Extra Rich Brownies	154
Josh's Bread Pudding	144
Lemon Mousse	42
Original Burnt Cream	86
Rice Custard Pudding	144
Trifle	160
Victor's Burnt Cream	180
Whiskey Balls	183

PIES

Chocolate Mousse Pie	138
Coconut Pie	148
Henry's Peanut Butter Cream Cheese Pie	112
Mocha Pecan Pie	18
Mud Pie	34
Raisin Cream Pie	132
Raspberry Bavarian Pie	54
Sally's Strawberry Truffle Pie	134

ETHNIC

Alu Gobi Curry	92
Fajitas	80
Joe's Fritata	124
Ražnjici	84
Souvlaka Arni	166
Salsa	140
Salsa de Aros Pollo	158
Salsa de Burrito	158